teach yourself

digital video and
pc editing
peter cope

The **teach yourself** series does exactly what it says, and it works. For over 60 years, more than 40 million people have learnt over 750 subjects the **teach yourself** way, with impressive results.

be where you want to be
with **teach yourself**

For UK order queries: please contact Bookpoint Ltd, 130 Milton Park, Abingdon, Oxon OX14 4TD. Telephone: +44 (0) 1235 827720. Fax: +44 (0) 1235 400454. Lines are open 09.00–18.00, Monday to Saturday, with a 24-hour message answering service. You can also order through our website www.madaboutbooks.com

For USA order queries: please contact McGraw-Hill Customer Services, P.O. Box 545, Blacklick, OH 43004-0545, USA. Telephone: 1-800-722-4726. Fax: 1-614-755-5645.

For Canada order queries: please contact McGraw-Hill Ryerson Ltd, 300 Water St, Whitby, Ontario L1N 9B6, Canada. Telephone: 905 430 5000. Fax: 905 430 5020.

Long renowned as the authoritative source for self-guided learning – with more than 30 million copies sold worldwide – the *Teach Yourself* series includes over 300 titles in the fields of languages, crafts, hobbies, business and education.

A catalogue entry for this title is available from The British Library.

Library of Congress Catalog Card Number: on file

First published in UK 2003 by Hodder Headline Ltd, 338 Euston Road, London, NW1 3BH.

First published in US 2003 by Contemporary Books, a Division of the McGraw Hill Companies, 1 Prudential Plaza, 130 East Randolph Street, Chicago IL 60601 USA.

This edition published 2003.

Typeset by Transet Limited, Coventry, England.
Printed in Great Britain for Hodder & Stoughton Educational, a division of Hodder Headline Ltd, 338 Euston Road, London NW1 3BH by Cox & Wyman Ltd, Reading, Berkshire.

Impression number   7 6 5 4 3 2 1
Year   2007 2006 2005 2004 2003

contents

The combination of personal computer and digital video camera is – so far as the movie maker is concerned – a match made in heaven. By combining the quality elements of the latter with the potency of the former, movie-making possibilities that would have previously demanded professional level equipment and high budgets come within the reach of almost everyone.

But there is still a perception that the process of crafting a good movie is difficult. While it is true that the creation of a polished product is something that requires practice and a degree of learnt skill, more modest movies that outshine anything that you could have created previously are simple.

Through this book we look at all aspects of digital video and video production. We'll come to understand what a digital video camera is capable of and why it is such a powerful tool. We'll see how easy it is to use video editing software. And this *really* is the case: video editing software – at least that designed for the video enthusiast – is a model of simplicity, using such simple constructional elements that it is child's play to use.

Later we'll look at how we can embellish our production by, for example, adding special effects (both visual and audible) and how we can set about crafting a movie production. We'll look at some of the practicalities involved if, say, we were commissioned to produce a video of a wedding or other event.

But underpinning much of what we'll discuss will be the importance of enjoying creating digital videos. In creating a digital movie we may not be aiming to produce the next blockbuster but we can create something that our friends and families can enjoy and – better still – give them the chance to share and relive important events.

01

what is digital video?

In this chapter you will learn:
- about differences in analogue and digital video
- why digital video is so effective a medium
- about the basics of movie making.

Video photography is often considered a relatively recent phenomenon born from the boom in consumer electronics of the late 1980s and 1990s. But contemporary video photographers represent the latest in a lineage that began with the film-based cine enthusiasts of the first half of the twentieth century. Inspired by film and movie makers of the early cinema industry, their skills were learnt the hard way. They battled with cumbersome and unforgiving equipment based on what was then regarded as the 'small' professional format, 16mm. It was not an activity for the faint hearted. If you could manage the camera's considerable physical burden, running costs would strongly test your finances. Hardware was very much considered a luxury and film was similarly expensive, not to mention scarce.

Despite these hurdles there were plenty of enthusiasts and aspiring filmmakers to make the medium flourish. Indeed, such was the demand that it led manufacturers to introduce 'amateur' equipment based upon a more economical 9.5mm wide film format (first seen in the early 1920s) and later the 'miniature' 8mm. The latter in particular proved a great success and though not capable of delivering great quality proved sufficient to bring many more enthusiasts into the fold. With the introduction of Super-8, which offered preloaded film cassettes and simplified operation, cine photography became truly popular and the cine camera became *de rigueur* at any social event or Mediterranean holiday.

Early video cameras aped the 16mm film forebears in both size and cost. The first models were shoulder carried and housed full size VHS or Betamax cassettes, putting video photography firmly back in the camp of the committed – and fit – enthusiast. But it took very little time for more compact equipment to appear and the bonus of being able to replay movies through a television (rather than a hastily erected screen and projector) meant that the days of cine were numbered.

These video cameras proved one of the great successes in home electronics that, in turn fuelled the development of smaller and better specified cameras. Diminutive one-piece camcorders, using the small Video-8 cassette or trimmed down VHS-C format, abounded and were soon joined by models offering improved quality – the so-called Hi-Band models. Combining improved recording methods with high quality video tape these newcomers offered impressive performance. Moreover, the improved performance meant video *editing* was now credible.

Editing had remained the unique selling point for cine photography and now this too was being challenged by the newcomer.

Editing using pre-digital formats was no easy matter and could test the patience and voracity of the most committed enthusiast. The nature of analogue video also meant that copying – an important process in editing – could result in quality shortfalls. It would take the arrival of digital video formats to make editing, by comparison, easy and more effective.

Though digital video is not new – professional users have had the option of using digital video equipment since the early 1990s – the change from older *analogue* video formats represents a very significant change in both the technology and the philosophy. No longer was size synonomous with quality; the most diminutive digital models could out perform any consumer – an many a pro – analogue model. And the option of convenient and effective editing using a computer made the format appeal to both the committed enthusiast and the more casual user.

Today digital video is quite firmly in the mainstream; a potent tool whether your aspirations are saving memories, creating blockbusters or even providing broadcast quality footage for your local TV news station. Armed with a digital camera, computer and video editing software you really have the capability to create a desktop movie studio.

Analogue and digital video compared

Despite the inroads digital video has made, analogue video is still the most common type of video system. Analogue comprises not only the formats used in pre-digital camcorders but also those of the majority of home videocassette recorders. And, far from being a dead (or even dying) format, new models of domestic recorder and video camera are appearing regularly even if in both cases they increasingly comprise the budget part of the market.

The key distinction between analogue and digital video is in how the vision and sound information is recorded on tape. An analogue format records this data as a continuously varying signal representing directly the brightness and colour of every point in a scene as the image is scanned (like the television

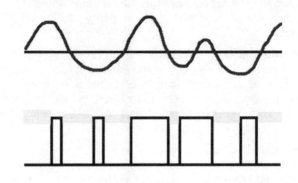

analogue signal (upper) and digital

picture that will ultimately display our video, the scene is recorded as a series of horizontal lines that build up the entire picture).

The mechanics of a digital video recording are very similar but rather than a continuously varying signal, the brightness and colour of every point in the image is converted into a digital code – a string of 0s and 1s – and this code is recorded on tape.

Though, in principle, both methodologies result in the same information being recorded on tape, recording the signal digitally makes it more robust. It is less prone to degradation when, for example, the video tape wears and, similarly, digital tapes can be copied and edited without compromising image quality. Copying analogue tape results in degraded images with the degradation visible even after a single copy.

So does this render those analogue recordings we may already have useless and preclude analogue video being edited digitally? Fortunately not – particularly for those of us with large collections of analogue tape. We shall see later that means exist for converting analogue recordings into digital ones.

The case for digital

The case for using digital video is absolutely compelling. Let's examine why.

digital video offers better than double the resolution of analogue

Quality

For most users quality is the principal determining factor in choosing a video format. And here digital video (DV) scores highest, offering picture quality that is, for all but the most discerning of users, indistinguishable from that produced by professional broadcast-grade equipment. Table 1 puts this into some kind of perspective. Conventional formats such as VHS and the camcorder offspring VHS-C take bottom positions. Video picture resolution is often quoted in lines. This has nothing to do with the number of picture lines that comprise the picture (625 in the case of PAL, 525 for NTSC) but rather the number of vertical lines that can be resolved. This is a somewhat better indication of the discernable detail in a video picture.

VHS struggles to achieve a rather unimpressive 240 lines but domestic digital formats can manage around 500. This puts picture quality in an entirely different league.

Table 1

Video format	Maximum lines of resolution
VHS, VHS-C	240
Video-8	275
Hi-8, SVHS	400
MicroMV	500
DV (MiniDV, Digital8)	500+

Though we'd have to consider other parameters – such as lens quality – before making any overall quality judgements, it's clear that DV begins streets ahead. It also means a humble domestic digital video camera is capable of results that can honestly be described as near broadcast quality.

Longevity

It is of little consequence if a VHS recording of Indiana Jones wears out after a few viewings; if we are not already tired of the movie, we can record it again at the next showing. But that VHS recording of a wedding or other meaningful event cannot be replaced. We want to be sure that we can still watch important and memorable events in the future. It is a sad but inevitable fact that recording media – and tape-based media in particular – are somewhat ephemeral and the recordings on them more so.

The good news is that the digital video signal is more resilient to the processes that cause degradation in analogue media. While tape wear degrades (or at least takes the edge off) recordings after only a few plays, digital recordings can survive considerably more wear. Other than physical failure (such as damage to a tape cassette) you should find that generations to come will be able to enjoy your movie making efforts. You may need to copy your treasured recording at some point in the future and for particular treasured recordings might make an identical second copy as a 'back-up' – much as you would important computer data. In years to come we will undoubtedly have the opportunity to copy those important recordings to a format that is more robust and resilient than anything available today.

analogue video suffers loss of resolution and quality after only a couple of copies

Copying

We mentioned above that analogue video (certainly so far as domestic systems are concerned) will show obvious degradation after one or two copies. In the language of video we use the term 'generation' rather than copies. An original video tape is known as the first generation or 'generation one'; copies made from this are generation two. Digital tape can be copied almost indefinitely without the quality suffering at all. We use the caveat *almost* because ultimately even digital recordings are subject to the effects of wear. After around 20 generations minor dropouts – small white flecks – can be expected. This is of no real consequence as, thanks to the desktop editing procedure, we need rarely go beyond third generation and often only to the second.

Editing

With a medium that has the quality and longevity of digital video and the ability to be easily copied it becomes viable – if not necessary – to edit it. There are many reasons why we would want to do this.

First, we might want to remove and discard superfluous material. Virtually every recording we make includes scenes or parts of scenes that are irrelevant. Think of all that movie footage of your feet, recorded when you forgot to press the pause button. Second, we might need to rearrange the order of some scenes to make our movie 'tell a story'. Or we might want to enliven the video with some titles and special effects.

Each of us will have our own reasons and needs for editing but in choosing digital video as the medium we have taken away many of the practical obstacles to successful editing and can concentrate more on the creative elements.

Better still, when we transfer a video recording to the computer for editing we are no longer limited to producing a simple edited copy. We can also, for example:

- *Compress the video to use on a website or send as an email attachment.* Video recordings, when transferred to a computer, produce very large files of data that are impractical to email. However, we can use specialized techniques to compress the original video signal to make it smaller and hence more practical to send. Compression involves trimming some of the data from our video but in a way that does not

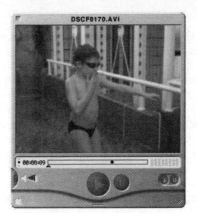

your video can also be replayed on any computer

unduly affect the video itself, though greater amounts of compression will compromise picture quality. We can, though, control and vary the degree of compression to balance the needs of quality and compactness.

- *Record it onto a conventional CD-ROM for distribution to other computer users.* CD-ROMs give us the chance to distribute our digital video files either in a 'raw' format or, for lengthier movies, in a compressed form. We can create the CD in a way that can be played on virtually any computer.

- *Add still digital images to produce slideshows along with our movie footage.* We can mix still images and movies in the same production, even creating slideshows which, using the same tools as for editing video material, can be treated with special effects.

- *Extract still images from movie footage for printing.* Equally, we can extract still frames from our movies and treat them as we might a still image from a digital stills camera. We can use image editing software to enhance or manipulate the image and then print it out.

- *Create DVDs and VideoCDs that can be replayed on domestic DVD players.* VideoCDs use a compression method that enables a reasonable amount of video to be squeezed onto a conventional CD and replayed on an ordinary DVD player. We can use this as an alternative method of distributing our finished movies. With suitable hardware we can even save the movie as a high-quality DVD Video and

the availability of DVD recorders and DVD recording media has made this a
credible distribution method for your productions

introduce special features (such as interactive menus and navigations) just like commercial offerings.

Throughout the course of this book we will look more closely at all of these options.

Sound performance

Sound is an important part of any video production and contributes significantly to the overall experience.

On the presumption that 'if the picture is good, no one will notice the awful sound' the first analogue videotapes featured narrow audio tracks (along the delicate tape edge) capable of sound quality no better than an audio cassette. Only some years later – as demand from increasingly sophisticated television sound systems rose – was the specification improved to offer FM radio quality sound.

The sound encoded with digital video is far superior and on paper is at least on a par with audio CD quality. Digital video's sampling rate (the number of samples of sound that are taken per second) at 48kHz is somewhat higher (better) than CD's 44.1kHz rate. More samples give greater sound fidelity. Perceived quality will ultimately be determined (and on occasions compromised) by other factors such as the microphones used and recording system in the camera. In practice, just think of digital video sound as very good.

Linear and non-linear editing

You'll sometimes hear the process of editing digital video on the computer described as Non-linear Editing or NLE. Data files – scenes of a video, for example – are stored somewhat randomly on the computer disc and can then be reconstructed into a continuous movie in whatever order we choose. The corresponding term Linear Editing describes the process – often used in analogue video editing – of copying scenes one by one in the edited order from a host video player to a destination video recorder. Quality concerns aside, linear editing is a much slower process.

The art of making movies

Of course we all have our favoured use for the video camera. For some it is a constant companion, used to record every detail of daily life. Others reserve it for special occasions, or perhaps holidays. Whatever your preference, making a movie is more than just recording a series of scenes and replaying them to ourselves or an audience. Movie making is a craft. Hence, as we progress through this book we'll also be looking at:

- Getting the best from the hardware. A thorough understanding of the camera and computer will lead to better results and make our working practices easier and swifter.
- Editing on a computer. Using a computer and the essential software for editing and embellishing our movie footage is remarkably simple (and is arguably easier than using image editing software) but some of the concepts may be a little unfamiliar. We'll look in detail at the methodology and explain any abstract concepts.
- Producing a movie. As we've just mentioned, turning raw footage into a movie is something of a craft but few of the skills involved are difficult to acquire. We'll look not only at the visuals, but also at the soundtrack and creative elements such as continuity and storytelling. We'll look at working on location and develop storyboards for movies and shooting lists for filming documentary and events.

- Recording events. There is nothing more dispiriting than viewing a video of an event, say, to find a crucial or memorable scene has been forgotten. The best man's speech at a wedding, the loyal toast at a dinner or even a child's lines in the school play. We'll see how forward planning is the key to a successful recording.

We'll also explore all the uses for your video camera and newly acquired movie making skills from business to purely creative. Many instructive manuals have mentioned the use of domestic hardware in the creation of *The Blair Witch Project*. While we may not all have the desire or skill to emulate this (as many wannabee follow-ups have shown) it does show that equipment need no longer be a limiting factor in the quality of video production.

The creative steps

Whatever the movie we intend to produce, whether a short presentation for delivery over the Web or the next blockbuster, the creative process will be the same. Here's a brief rundown of the stages and the processes – both creative and practical – required at each.

Pre-production

Successful movie making depends on good planning, and planning is the crux of the pre-production phase.

Pre-production usually begins with an outline. This contains your very first ideas about the movie. Depending on the complexity of the production you may need to elaborate on the outline, producing a script that details the shots required, any additional resources including voiceover narrations (where appropriate) and the sound track.

An excellent way of visualizing the script is to draw up a storyboard. Storyboards are sketches (which are for your eyes only, so do not have to be works of art!) that show each scene in the production as you wish it to be filmed. Though cartoon-like in presentation it is a great way to work out the shots required along with any special instructions for each. If you are new to movie making, you may find that storyboards are a better bet than written scripts.

Production

The production phase sees us recording all those scenes that we have been storyboarding. It is probably the briefest of the three stages, but is nonetheless crucial. This is where your pre-production efforts pay off. Get it wrong and no amount of post-production work can put it right!

Other media, such as still images (that you might use later for titles or other effects) can be recorded now, as can elements of the sound track (though the complete sound track might contain material procured during pre-production and post-production).

Post-production

This is all about turning the raw footage and other media into a coherent movie. It's about editing video clips and sequencing – putting into order. It's about adding sound and effects. And it's about distributing your masterpiece to an expectant audience, whether friends, family, work colleagues or anyone who uses the Internet.

In the course of this book we'll take a slightly different path through these processes. True to our brief of digital video editing we'll look first at the processes of getting digital video footage to the desktop and how that material is edited. We'll then explore how we can use the tools at our disposal to enrich the production.

Taking this approach places us in a more informed position when it comes to planning and executing a production. We will be well versed in the needs of the editing process and have a better understanding of the shots needed.

Video editing without a computer

We've described the PC as an integral element of digital video production. But is this necessarily true? No. There is an alternative that actually predates current digital video editing systems. This is the dedicated video editor.

Led by models such as MacroSystem's Casablanca, these devices are capable of achieving much that a PC editing system can but have the benefit – important to many users who are not confident using computers – of being particularly easy to use.

video editing systems make a viable – if restricted – alternative to PC systems

The drawback is that most of these comprise 'closed' systems. Whereas a computer-based system can be upgraded with new hardware or software (and additional resources, such as new effects, added) video editing machines are more difficult to upgrade in either way. They are also 'one trick ponies'. A computer is limited only by the software applications loaded on it. Your video editing PC can also be word processor, image editing station and more; the dedicated video editor can edit video footage and no more.

A machine like Casablanca's best selling *Avio* is nonetheless very well specified. A typical onboard 20GB hard disc, like that on a computer, can store up to 13 hours of video, depending on the quality required. It can also record from analogue or digital cameras. Scenes can be edited, transitions added between and titles generated. And once your work is finished the movie can be output – again via analogue or digital connections.

02

getting started

In this chapter you will learn
- about the basics of the digital video camera
- about computer and software requirements
- all about the software we'll be using through the book.

A comprehensive desktop studio requires very little equipment and certainly far less than that required to make a similarly specified production using analogue tape. Whereas analogue video editing requires twin video recorder decks, sound and vision mixers, title generators and more your whole digital movie studio need comprise only three essentials: camera, computer and video editing software.

Let's take a look at these along with some of those extras that are normally classed as 'accessories' but that most users will class as essentials.

The camera

If you are new to the video world the first recommended purchase is the camera. Even if you don't have a computer yet, or have a computer but not the appropriate software, you'll want to start recording video *now*. Why? Just think of those events, perhaps a birth, wedding or even a school play that can never happen again. With a camera in hand you can capture these memories even if the editing has to wait a while.

We're being deliberately brief here as we'll be looking at the digital video camera in considerably more depth in the following chapter. For the moment it is worth commenting that the digital camera market is now a mature one. Models exist to cater for just about every need from those requiring a simple, pocketable device to those intent on producing their own

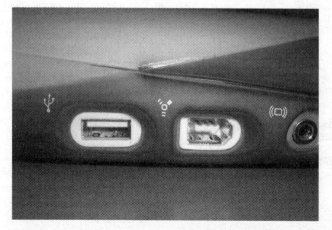

the FireWire connection is essential for downloading direct from the camera

blockbuster. Whatever the size and whatever other features it boasts the ideal digital video camera will have a FireWire (sometimes known by the less glamorous systematic name of IEEE 1394) connector for the essential task of transferring signals (copying video) to the computer. It is very desirable that this is a two-way connection. The edited video can then be copied back (via the camera) to tape.

Power

Like their still camera stablemates digital video cameras have a voracious appetite for power. Power is needed to drive the tape mechanism, viewfinder (or LCD) display panel (along with the zoom and focus mechanisms) and without it you are stuck. And nothing is more frustrating than being at that once-in-a-lifetime event with a dead camera. Hence your kitbag should always contain at least one fully charged spare battery. Modern rechargeable batteries are much less fickle than their predecessors and can provide a reliable amount of power for a reasonable length of time – some even feature monitors that display (via LEDs) the amount of remaining charge. It makes sense to include the battery charger too, so that you can top up the power when convenient.

Tape

Don't forget the importance of carrying some spare tape. You may not plan to shoot much video on any particular day or at an event, but you can rest assured that something extra special will occur just after you have run out of tape. And, though the chances are commendably slight, tape cassettes do fail. In such a case you might lose the footage you've just recorded, but you can at least gain partial compensation by getting some new recording.

The computer

Whether you already own a computer or are shopping for a new one, let's consider the key components, looking particularly closely at them in the context of video editing.

The Central Processing Unit

The heart of any computer is its central processing unit (CPU). This is often colloquially referred to as the computer's 'brain' as it is where the mathematical calculations are performed. Anything we do with a computer – including video manipulations – involves complex and extensive mathematical computations and it is the speed at which these can be performed that is the most significant element in determining the 'speed' or performance of the computer.

Just about every Windows computer uses one of the Pentium family of CPUs, or an equivalent from other manufacturers. As a general rule it is fair to say that the faster the *clock speed* of the Pentium chip, the better the performance. Measured in megahertz (millions of cycles per second) and gigahertz (thousands of millions of cycles per second) this speed determines how fast calculations can be performed. The overall computer performance will be somewhat less than this speed – it will depend upon the performance of other components and that of the system (known as the 'bus') used to pass data around.

Macintosh computers use the PowerPC processor family, with G3 and G4 versions in widespread use. The somewhat different design of the PowerPC processor means that clock speeds are not equivalent to those of Windows PCs. Though (again) it is not a simple matter to address, as so many variables affect the equation, Macintosh computers will have a clock speed of roughly half that of a similarly specified (and performing) Windows PC.

Memory

We use the term memory confusingly to describe two distinct and separate parts of the computer.

The first is the space on a computer's hard disc drive available to store data, whether applications, documents, images or video. When an application is installed on your computer it is written to the memory on the hard disc; when we save a documents – a piece of correspondence for example – created in a word processing application, it is written to this memory. Similarly, when images or movies are downloaded from digital cameras and digital video cameras respectively, the image and movie files are stored here. You can think of this as your library: this is where your computer will go to find data when you ask it to open a particular file or application.

Once that file or application is opened it will be stored in the computer's other memory resource, the RAM. Short for Random Access Memory, this is a solid state (i.e. it has no moving parts) memory area to which information that is being processed by the computer's CPU can be written to and from very fast. Think of this as a holding area, where the information that is needed, or likely to be needed, for use with the current tasks can be held ready for immediate use.

For best performance you'll need plenty of both RAM and hard disc memory. A large hard disc (and one that has plenty of free space) is essential for storing digital video downloaded from the computer. When, with digital video we typically handle files (representing scenes from the video) that are hundreds of megabytes in size.

memory chips such as this are an important element in computer performance

For processing the video, which includes manipulating the order of scenes, adding titles and applying effects (such as smooth transitional fades between scenes) we need extensive amounts of RAM. The software manufacturer's requirements are a good indication of what is needed, but often these address the minimum requirement, rather than a typical. It is wise to have at least twice this amount. Don't forget that other processes – such as running the computer's operating system – can consume quite a bit of the RAM and would otherwise compromise that available for the editing application.

If your computer is short of RAM, but otherwise well specified you can, in most cases, add more. Any computer store will be able to supply you with additional RAM chips (and will ensure that you are supplied with the correct type for your computer). Fitting additional RAM varies from the simple (in the case of most Macintosh models) to the extremely difficult (mostly on older computers). Again, many vendors offer a fitting service that will include testing that the new memory works and is recognized by the computer.

Should you need additional hard disc space then there are a number of options, including replacement or adding a second disc, which we look at on page 21.

Monitors

The monitor is the part of the computer that displays documents, images and, in our case, will act as a movie editing screen. There are two types: CRT (or cathode ray tube) types are physically similar to conventional television tubes. They are economically priced, offer great quality but can, especially with the larger tube sizes, take up a substantial part of your desk.

LCD panels offer compact design with excellent performance

LCD (liquid crystal display) panels are increasingly popular as they offer a large, flat display that boasts a thickness of around 5cm – ideal when space is at a premium. Early models lagged behind equivalent CRT models both in terms of image quality and – important for photographic applications – colour fidelity. Both these limitations have now been addressed and LCD panels can offer great quality. An increasing number of computer systems are now supplied with LCD panels as standard.

What is the ideal size of monitor? Most commentators will say, given that all quality issues were equal, biggest is best. While in an ideal world this is absolutely true there are practical considerations to be borne in mind. Monitors of 22 inches (screen sizes, somewhat strangely for a high technology industry, are still expressed in inches and refer to the size of the screen diagonal) are fantastic, enabling the sometimes crowded interface of video editing software to be best displayed. The drawback is that such screens usually cost somewhat more than double a screen half the size.

A 17-inch CRT monitor is now standard and will be supplied with the computer system, alternatively it will be a 15-inch LCD panel (a size which offers much the same working area). For video editing applications either of these screens will be quite sufficient.

It is important to note that a larger screen will not necessarily give you a larger workspace unless the *resolution* of the screen is set appropriately. The screen resolution defines how much information can be displayed on the screen. Measured in pixels (picture cells, the smallest unit on the computer screen), typical resolutions are 800 × 600 (probably the lowest for practical purposes) and 1024 × 768.

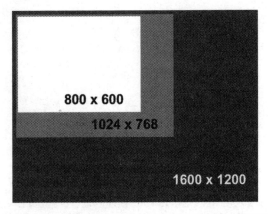

the larger the screen resolution, the more 'desktop' that can be displayed at any one time

If we were writing about digital still photography we would be somewhat more concerned with the issue of colour fidelity: when editing digital images we need to be sure that the colour of the images we are editing onscreen is very close to that which will be printed out on our printer. This is less of an issue with digital video editing, but no excuse to have an incorrectly calibrated monitor. Calibration routines are included in many operating systems or with some monitors. It makes sense to use them.

Sound

For most computer users the audio reproduction is of somewhat secondary importance. True, it is useful for playing audio CDs as you work or (with the appropriate subwoofer attached) delivering knee-trembling vibrations as you play the latest video game but otherwise it can be considered superfluous.

Not so for the video photographer. As we've noted already the sound track of your video is an important element so we need to ensure that we are able to reproduce sound in a fitting manner. Most computer systems now come with sound systems that are well up to the task in hand. If not, such systems can be purchased easily – in many stores you can audition your shortlist to compare quality. Do be aware, however, that if you have a Windows PC and no speakers, you may need to add a sound card to the computer before you can connect speakers. All Macintosh computers include sound systems as standard; in the case of desktop machines (including 'classic' and LCD iMac models) these are excellent for editing purposes. Though laptops are sound enabled the speakers are somewhat small and may benefit being replaced with something more meaty.

As an alternative to speaker systems (and particularly if you like being immersed in really loud sound) consider using headphones. You can choose from a range of models specifically designed for the purpose, although most models deliver quite acceptable performances.

Hard drives

If you plan to produce a minor epic on your computer you may find that the amount of video you need to transfer to your computer will be greater than the hard disc space available. You can add more space in several ways. The most obvious (but not necessarily the most successful) is to clear your hard disc of any applications or files that are redundant or little used. Back up anything that might be important before removing it. If your disc is already as clear as possible then you need to consider an alternative.

Many computers will have space for adding a second hard drive. This is fitted into a space within the main computer enclosure (often called an expansion bay). Once fitted the new drive will appear on your computer monitor's screen in exactly the same way as the original disc.

Some computers do not have such space or may have another device (such as a FireWire card) already installed. For these and also laptop computers (that rarely have the space for an additional internal drive) there are external drives that can be connected via one of the standard connectors. For speed of communication it is advisable to select a FireWire model. Most FireWire drives also take their power from the FireWire connector, reducing the amount of connections necessary. Many are also pocketable so can be used, for example, for transporting files between an office and home computer. To reduce the load on the FireWire system it's a good idea to use an external FireWire disc for your other applications, leaving your main hard disc for storing files from your camera. Copying digital video from the camera to an external drive via the computer's FireWire system can result in occasional glitches and dropouts in the video.

an external disc is an ideal way of extending capacity

Note that it is also possible to replace the main (or only) hard disc of a computer with a compatible model of greater capacity. This can be a DIY job, but as the process involves reinstalling and reconfiguring software you may prefer to leave it to your dealer.

Recordable media drives

Recordable/re-recordable CD drives are increasingly becoming the norm on even the most lowly of computers and such a drive makes backing up simple. With capacities of up to 700MB you can store a great deal of data. Though even this is insufficient for all but the briefest of digital video clips, you can use them to record VideoCDs.

Although not as commonplace, recordable DVD drives are well suited to recording digital video and creating your own DVD videos. Software such as DVDit! (Windows) and iDVD (Macintosh) have made DVD creation (almost) as simple as digital video editing.

adding a DVD drive allows video productions to be output to DVD Video discs

Connectivity

The essential FireWire connection is not standard on all Windows PCs but many third-party FireWire cards can be purchased and provide this connectivity. Some video editing applications are now supplied with the respective card, along with easy installation instructions. Installation is usually quite straightforward, though if you are wary about opening up your computer many of the bigger computer stores will install cards purchased from them for a modest charge.

FireWire cards are easily available and easily fitted

Recommended systems

Such has been the escalation in the power and speed (the critical features for digital video) over the last few years that most home and office computers are suitable for video editing. Table 2 gives the PC and Mac specifications quoted for the two popular editing applications for the respective computer types, Roxio's *VideoWave* and Apple's *iMovie*.

Table 2

	VideoWave (Windows)	iMovie (Macintosh)
Min Processor/Speed	Pentium III / 800MHz	G3 / 300MHz
RAM Memory	128MB	128MB
Disc space (program)*	110MB	20MB
Operating System	Windows 98, 2000, Me, XP	MacOS 8.1 (or later), OSX

*Depends on the amount of supplementary material provided

For Macintosh users we can cut through most of those specifications by saying that if you've a G3 (300MHz) or faster processor, along with an on-board FireWire connection, you're all set. You'll probably also find (if you dig around with the installation CDs that accompanied your computer) that a copy of iMovie is included and can be installed in minutes.

PC users (with later versions of Windows, including Me and XP) will find Windows Movie Maker included. Though ostensibly a similar program to iMovie it is somewhat more restricted for our purposes. We do, however, take an overview of its capabilities in Chapter 18.

The best PC?

There has been an ongoing debate for many years about which is the better computer: the Macintosh or Windows PC. In practice that question is largely irrelevant as we tend to be governed by the computer we have, or that which we feel more comfortable with.

It is probably true that the Macintosh, a computer that was built from the ground up to handle graphical displays and has an internal structure that reflects this, has the edge. But, in a head to head contest differences are likely to be slight. Windows users score with the range of applications (including video editing programs) available to them. If you are a seasoned user of Windows – in any of its flavours – you need not feel handicapped in any way and fluency with either operating system is the more important asset.

Note that throughout this book we use the term 'PC' to describe any personal computer, whether Mac or Windows driven.

Software

The video editing software is the final part of the digital jigsaw. Though such products have been around for some time by virtue of the needs of the professional video studios they tended to be high priced and high specification.

This all changed largely due to the arrival of the original iMovie software from Apple. The company had previously launched their own high-end product, Final Cut Pro, but iMovie was designed specifically for the enthusiast market. It made the logical assumption that such users would have had no (or very little) previous knowledge of movie editing in any form but might want to make an enjoyable movie from their raw recordings. Even though simplicity in use was the paramount design criterion iMovie has proved that credible movies can be made simply. By cutting away the complexities of previous products the result is a very useful tool indeed.

Market demand has led to further applications appearing covering a wide range of needs from the very basic through to the broadcast professional. These can be divided into three market segments that I have given the crude definitions of enthusiast, intermediate level and high level.

Enthusiast applications

Though not meant for intensive professional or semi-professional movie making projects, enthusiast-level applications are commendably well specified yet feature interfaces and controls that are easy to use and navigate. Many, including iMovie and VideoWave, feature interfaces that are metaphors for everyday devices such as videocassette recorders, with the controls aping those of these devices. Hence the newcomer tends to feel reasonably at home. These products tend to feature an elementary video construction method where the timeline (the graphical representation of the movie) is somewhat rudimentary, with video clips, effects and titles being simply dragged and dropped on. However, these applications provide all the functionality for most movie making projects.

VideoWave, for example, enables:

- the import of digital video and (with appropriate hardware) analogue
- simple drag and drop non-linear editing
- the addition of titles, special effects and soundtracks
- the output of finished material to a videotape, CD or DVD.

Though often referred to as beginner products, the term low-end is more appropriate. Even though they are basic and easy to use it is still possible to produce quite credible movies with them.

Other products that fit this category include Ulead's VideoStudio and ArcSoft's VideoImpression.

ArcSoft's VideoImpression shows the drag and drop simplicity of these products

Intermediate-level applications

Intermediate-level packages are usually characterized by more elaborate timelines. The applications tend to be simplified versions of more elaborate packages and feature more workmanlike interfaces. You'll find these include extended ranges of titling options and special effects. You will also be able to handle a greater range of video file formats (for example DV, MPEG1, MPEG2 and AVI) with the ability to import or export in any combination.

Exemplars of this group include Edit DV, DV EditStudio and Dazzle MainActor.

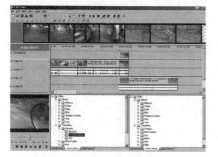

EditStudio is typical of the intermediate-level packages available

High-level applications

High-level packages (a term that is more appropriate than either 'serious' or 'professional') include the minimum features that a professional video producer would expect, though most applications tend to pack in somewhat more than this minimum. In these you would expect to have:

- twin monitor screens (rather than the single, multipurpose screen offered by other applications)
- batch capture of clips (video clips or scenes are automatically collected and listed)
- multiple video and audio track timeline
- a comprehensive set of filters, effects and titling tools.

For most users this category is characterized by Adobe's Premiere. Although it has not achieved the same dominance in its market segment as the same company's image editing application Photoshop, it is very widely used. And availability in near identical Windows and Macintosh versions makes it the ideal choice for many video production houses. Despite professional credentials Premiere is used by many enthusiasts and, unless your specific requirements are particularly obtuse, is likely to provide all the tools you are likely to need.

If you are familiar with Photoshop, you'll know it features an 'open' design that permits additional third party 'plug-ins'.

These are small applications that work seamlessly with the host to provide additional features, typically effects filters. Premiere features a similarly open design. This adds to the appeal to professionals. They know if Premiere can't do something, there will be a plug-in that might.

If you envisage a need for this level of package other names to watch out for include Final Cut Pro (Apple) and Xpress DV from Avid.

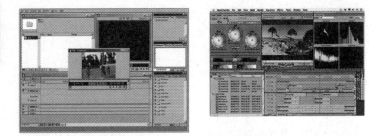

high-level packages feature comprehensive interfaces and very extensive feature sets

Rather like word processing applications, the key features are very similar no matter which product you use. Hence, in most of our work we'll be using VideoWave and iMovie yet the processes and techniques used work – often in a very similar manner – no matter what application you may be using. We have chosen these two products on account of them being sufficiently well specified and also because their (very clearly laid out) interfaces are representative of many other applications. Also VideoWave has the bonus of featuring its own interface that, although Windows compliant, looks identical no matter which version of Windows is in use on the host computer. We'll also bring in other applications – such as those designed for creating audio or DVDs for example - when needed.

VideoWave: the interface

The VideoWave interface is divided into zones based around a metaphorical desktop called the Console.

1 The Library is where you'll find the media for a particular production. The Library would normally contain video clips (downloaded from the camcorder or stored on the computer hard disc) but can also contain images, sound files and music. You can click on the icons at the top of the Library panel to see alternate presentations of the media available; click on the pull-down menu to select a different set of files.

2 The monitor window (called the viewscreen in VideoWave) will display chosen video clips when selected from the Library and will play the assembled video from the Storyline. The lower part of this panel contains the edit controls, depicted as VCR controls. Below this is a timeslider that can be used for finding specific points in a video.

3 The Storyline is an interpretation of the traditional timeline that illustrates, by means of thumbnails, all the clips, transitions and effects used in the production as they have been sequenced.

4 Ranged along the left edge of the workspace are the Mode Selectors. Clicking on one of these selects editing functions such as Cutting Room (to cut and edit clips). Features relevant to each mode appear in the context sensitive part of the console, below the Library and Viewscreen panels.

5 Context-sensitive panel. Dialogue and informational boxes appear here according to the current activity.

iMovie: the interface

The iMovie interface is similar to that of VideoWave and includes comparable elements.

1 Like the Library in VideoWave the shelf stores the individual video clips. When a digital video is downloaded scenes are automatically separated and stored on the shelf as distinct video clips. Tabs at the base of the shelf allow you to open alternate panes that display (and select) Transitions, Titles, Effects or Audio Effects.

2 The monitor window displays the currently selected video clip or your movie, as assembled in the timeline.

3 Below the monitor window is the scrubber bar. This represents the current clip (or the entire movie) timewise. Moving the playhead (the triangular marker) enables a precise part of the clip (down to an individual frame) to be displayed. VCR-like buttons are provided below the scrubber bar, along with a Camera/Edit mode toggle switch.

4 The Timeline viewer shows the movie clips and audio tracks currently compiled in the production. Clicking on the eye tab changes the timeline to a Clip Viewer. In this display the clips are represented as thumbnails. Though this view is not as comprehensive, it is particularly useful when adding transitional effects.

5 Completing the desktop are a pair of icons. The first is a trash can to which unwanted clips can be dragged. The Disc Gauge

shows how much free disc remains available for adding further DV footage. The colour changes from green to yellow to red as the amount of disc space drops to 'low' and critical.

Analogue to digital converters

Here's one of those pieces of kit that does not comprise one of our core elements. And, depending on your standpoint, it will either be essential or utterly irrelevant. It all depends on whether you are new to digital video – and video movie making in general – or whether you are graduating from an earlier, analogue system. If you are one of the former, you can safely skip this section entirely; if the latter, read on!

Having owned or used video cameras of various vintages (and invariably of the analogue type) the question will arise 'Can I use material recorded with these for digital video editing?' Fortunately the answer is yes, but with the caveat that we will need to convert the signals first into a digital form.

The purpose of an analogue to digital converter is to convert analogue video into a digital signal that your computer can recognize and handle in the same way as that from a digital camcorder. Many of us have extensive archives of analogue tape recording that contain unrepeatable events that we wish to save for posterity and no doubt much of this will benefit from some judicious editing.

Many computer peripheral manufacturers offer converters and using them is a cinch. An analogue video source (such as a camcorder or home video recorder) is connected to one side of the device and the other is connected to the computer. When the analogue video is played the converter produces a digital output that is stored on the computer.

If you think you'll need one of these converters there are several models available such as Formac's Studio and Hollywood Bridge. Prices are around half what you would pay for a basic digital video camera.

If you have a smaller collection of old tapes and can't really justify the price of a converter you can have footage converted (and recorded on to digital videotape) by your local photography store.

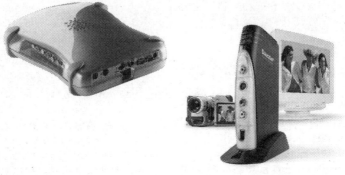

A to D converters such as Formac's Studio and Dazzle's Hollywood Bridge make the capture of analogue video (and even live TV) virtually as simple as digital video

Note that there are also cheaper converters, such as the CapSure USB from iRez, that can capture video of a slightly lower standard from most video sources (and even from live TV broadcasts, subject to copyright limitations). These are ideal for digitizing analogue video that is not intended for reproduction at the highest quality (for example, for email or website use). In Chapter 11 we'll be looking more closely at the capture of analogue material, including capture using USB devices.

USB capture devices may look like toys but are remarkably effective

Accessories

Whether you consider them essential or accessory, there are two more pieces of kit that can make your video productions even better.

Microphones

It is somewhat sad then that the manufacturers of video cameras (of all types, not just digital) are able to endow their creations with the finest in optical quality but pay only cursory attention to the audio hardware. Many built-in microphones offer only mediocre performance and it is not until we compare the results with those made with a more effective model that we notice the enormous quality gap.

External microphones are relatively cheap and can make a substantial improvement. You can choose between omnidirectional models (that are responsive to sounds from all directions) and unidirectional models (more sensitive to sounds broadly in front of the camera), which are ideal for applications that involve the recording of conversation. There are even 'zoom' models that record sound from a smaller, more precise area in front of the camera. Zoom microphones are particularly useful at isolating the sound of the subject area from general environmental 'noise'. We'll look at these and other models when we examine the best ways to record sound.

a zoom microphone

Tripods

Yes they are cumbersome, often clumsy and sometimes hard to set up – but absolutely essential for getting the best from your camera. Ask any camcorder owner whether they own a tripod and a sizeable number will say 'yes'. Ask those same people how many use them most of the time and the proportion will fall substantially. This is something of a shame as movies taken using a tripod prove eminently more watchable and appear more professional. A steady image is as important to the video photographer as a sharp, non-blurred image is to the still photographer.

It's a good idea to get into the habit of using a tripod, particularly when you are going 'on location' with the deliberate intention of collecting some movie footage. Many models are light, compact and easy to carry for long periods. The best models are those with pan and tilt heads, rather than the ball and socket type used for still cameras. Pan and tilt heads make levelling the camera easy and moving the camera so that it is always square on to the horizon is simple.

more an essential than an accessory, the tripod is the sure route to steady movies

If a tripod really is too cumbersome to take with you, or you are filming in an area where they are not permitted (perhaps for safety reasons) then look at improvised supports – benches, fences and walls are among those that can be pressed into service when necessary. Alternatively you can use a monopod. Doubling up as walking stick when not in use, it can often be an ideal compromise.

03

the digital video camera

In this chapter you will learn:
- how to choose a digital video camera
- which formats are best for you
- about the features of a digital video camera.

Apart from the word 'digital' there is nothing that overtly distinguishes a digital video camera from the host of models based upon earlier, analogue formats. Even if you were to peer inside (when changing a tape for example) you'd still be hard pressed to find any characteristics that set these cameras apart.

Like so much of the world that has embraced the digital revolution – television, mobile phones and pre-recorded video (DVD) – it is in the *quality* of the results that we see a clear difference. Television pictures are no longer affected by atmospheric or environmental limitations, mobile phones no longer demand that callers resort to shouting as the signal strength diminishes. So it is with digital video. Home movies with picture quality approaching that of broadcast television pictures. And the ability to edit those movies conveniently on computer.

In this section we'll look more closely at digital video cameras and, in particular, the features that make them uniquely suitable for computer-based editing. We'll also look at the principal camera features and make objective assessments of their value.

What is a digital video camera?

The world of broadcast television met its digital future in the early 1990s with the introduction of digital video cameras and editing facilities. It cost the broadcasters dearly but, at a stroke, they were repaid with a raft of powerful new production tools capable of delivering the finest quality with astonishing flexibility. They have never looked back.

The viewer, ironically, saw nothing of this revolution; they continued to receive their conventional television pictures oblivious of the fundamental changes at the television network centres. Digital television – the transmission system we know today - was yet to come.

Consumer digital video, though derived from professional systems, didn't debut until later in the decade. As with any new technology the first cameras to appear were very much premium, niche products with price tags pitched more to the pockets of the 'semi-pro' than the enthusiast. They also launched into a marketplace already divided between no less than four analogue camcorder formats - VHS-C, Video-8, SVHS-C and Hi-8.

Rather than adding to the confusion, the unique virtues of digital video were soon recognized and helped bring about critical acceptance of the format. Timing too was fortuitous. With televisions growing ever larger, many consumers began to realize the quality limitations of existing video formats. Digital video provided the solution. Not only did it offer picture quality to match the performance of their new televisions but it held the promise of a lot more besides.

The possibility of computer-based editing or desktop editing was one. The power of personal and small business computers was soaring as prices went into free fall. Digital video could soon be edited on such machines with no loss of quality. Every desktop had the capability to become a movie studio and every user (so the protagonists advised) had the chance to be the new Spielberg!

Buying a DV camcorder

If you're new to digital video or new to video photography, the choice in the marketplace can be quite baffling. It is further complicated because the tools offered by digital video editing applications supersede many of the features that were once important 'must haves' when shopping for a new camera. Hence we need to assess the criteria that would normally guide our purchase mindful of the opportunities offered by the software.

compact DV cameras are the most popular

semi-professional models offer more features but are somewhat larger

Formats

The term digital video camera is generally, though imprecisely, used to describe cameras that use the *miniDV* cassette. About half the size of an audio cassette and much the same dimensions as a DAT tape, these minuscule offerings enable ultra-compact camera design yet are still capable of delivering digital video quality recordings for up to an hour per tape. Cameras range from the tiny (smaller in volume than this book) to larger, shoulder mounted machines. As the details of the DV format are very precisely specified you'll find tapes recorded on one camcorder should easily replay on another without any adjustment (just try to find two VHS-C camcorders that are so identically configured!).

There are, however, alternate tape formats used in camcorders and also disc-based formats.

Digital8 tapes are identical in size to Video-8 tapes and somewhat larger than DV tapes. Both, however, are considerably smaller than analogue tapes

Digital8

Devised by Sony, Digital8 uses Video-8 or Hi-8 format tapes but records a digital signal identical to that recorded on a mini-DV tape. Though you might consider the appearance of another format as divisive, Digital8 has the unique advantage of compatibility with existing Video-8 and Hi-8 recordings.

Digital8 cameras match Video8 cameras in size but offer substantially better performance

Those with extensive collections of 'old' videotapes of these formats will recognize the immediate benefit of being able to retain and use those tapes in new productions. The drawback (which is not particularly significant) is the camera size. Dictated by the tape cassette, Digital8 models are somewhat larger than the corresponding miniDV models. You'll also find a smaller range of models available.

MicroMV

Sony has a knack of producing innovative yet idiosyncratic media – consider Betamax video, the Elcassette and MiniDisc for example. So it came as no surprise that, after releasing Digital8 it announced the MicroMV digital video format.

One of the rationales for this new format – that could otherwise have seemed, in marketing terms, likely to further fragment the marketplace – was to enable the building of cameras even smaller than the miniDV format allowed. MicroMV cassettes are more than 60 per cent smaller than the already tiny cassettes of the miniDV format. They also feature a memory chip that can store pertinent information regarding recordings, such as when the last shots were recorded, clip length and the remaining recording time. A still frame from up to 11 video clips can also be stored to enable a specific shot to be found easily.

A second is that by employing an alternate recording format – MPEG2 – that permits the more compact storage of data, less computer hard disc space is consumed when video material is transferred to the computer. MPEG2 is the same format used for the video component of DVD Video and the form employed for many of the world's digital television standards.

MicroMV cameras are truly pocketable

A bonus has been to achieve these reductions in physical and data size without unduly compromising picture or audio quality. Despite offering recording times on a par with miniDV tapes, only in low light conditions does picture quality suffer slightly in comparison with the other digital formats.

whatever the model, the tape heads and assemblies are tiny

Disc-based recording

For many users, a tape-based system is something of an anathema. When digital video offers so much in terms of quality and longevity are we entirely happy consigning the result to an ephemeral resource such as tape? Tape, as users have discovered since the earliest days of reel-to-reel audio recording, has with almost unnerving certainty a tendency to snap, wear or crumple. And by virtue of the tolerance of digital signals to wear (even a worn digital tape can be read with sufficient detail to render a good picture) there's often little warning of impending failure.

Hence most camcorder manufacturers now include a recordable DVD model in their line-up. DVD has many advantages as a recording medium but has been handicapped by differing recording formats that are often incompatible. However, there are good indications that DVD represents a strong future path for digital video recording. The meteoric uptake of DVD players in the home market makes the medium especially attractive. In terms of downloading recording to a computer, however, there is little difference between disc-based cameras and tape-based models.

If we are being particularly pedantic there are two further formats, variations on the DV format, known as DVCAM and DVPRO. Designed (and priced) as professional formats these use slightly different data compression regimes to achieve video source material that is a little more robust than 'basic' consumer DV. 'DV' in this book refers to the consumer version.

Lenses

Graduates to digital video from photographic backgrounds tend to put optical performance at the top of their list of specifications. Only with first rate optics, they will argue, can digital video deliver the quality of which it is ultimately capable.

Excepting only those high-end cameras (variously described as for the 'enthusiast' or 'semi-pro') that feature interchangeable lenses, like SLR stills cameras, all digital video cameras include built-in zoom lenses. Quality is invariably good.

Don't, though, be seduced by camera manufacturers who tend to play a cunning numbers game. In their unending quest for market dominance these manufacturers specify zoom ratios as great as 100x or even more. This is, sadly, something of a contrivance. These cameras actually feature lenses that have an *optical* zoom of more modest proportions - 10x or even 20x. This is no mean ratio in itself and equivalent to, for those familiar with 35mm camera terminology, a 35mm – *700mm* zoom!

The extended ratios are due to some electronic trickery called digital zooming. By enlarging the centre part of the digitally acquired image these enormous magnifications become possible – but at a cost. Putting aside the artefacts introduced by such magnification (exaggerated camera shake and narrow field of view) enlarging a small part of the imaging chip caused such a dire loss of resolution that quality immediately and very obviously suffers. The benefits of digital video are immediately lost.

Digital zoom ratios are best treated with a degree of scepticism. Look for a good optical zoom range and treat the digital extension as a bonus.

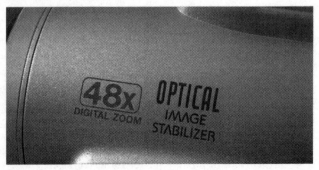

electronic zoom ratios are less significant than other features, such as stabilizers

Image stabilizers

An enhancement that is definitely of value is a Digital Image Stabilizer, sometimes called the Electronic Image Stabilizer. We mentioned earlier that the tripod should be regarded as something more than an accessory. But even the most devoted enthusiast has no wish to carry a tripod – or even a monopod – everywhere. This is where image stablization features can come to the rescue.

Image stabilizers counteract much of the shake (due to the small involuntary movements of our hands) by monitoring the camera image and compensating for any small transient motion. It's not a total solution: larger movements can't be compensated for and even small movements, when amplified by using a zoom lens at its most extreme setting, will still appear.

Some cameras offer *optical* image stabilizers. Relying on a complex fluid-filled prism system these often give better results but command a price premium.

Neither type is foolproof. If you're deliberately panning the camera (horizontally or vertically) for example, the stabilizer can sometimes misinterpret this as shake and compensate accordingly. Your reward is a distinctly juddery pan. In such circumstances you would be advised to turn off the feature (both electronic and optical versions can be turned on or off).

Viewfinders

Camcorder viewfinders began by aping their professional cousins and including a tiny electronic screen. Initially black and white, this little screen gave a good indication of the image being recorded on tape. Those screens now tend to be colour and have been augmented by LCD panel displays.

Using the same technology as 'pocket' televisions, these LCD screens swing out from the camera body and can be tilted and pivoted to allow the user an optimum view. No longer does the filmmaker need to squint through a viewfinder firmly attached to the camera – he or she can use the camera overhead, on the ground or wherever and still be able to preview the shot.

Add a tiny speaker and the LCD screen doubles up as a replay system. You can review your movie immediately after recording, complete with sound and vision.

the fold-out viewscreen is an excellent feature – except in bright sunlight

The weakness of LCD screens is the tendency for the image to be swamped by bright ambient light. Even average sunlight upon them causes the image to disappear. They can also prove an onerous drain on your camera's battery. In such situations the conventional viewfinder comes back into its own.

Connectivity

All cameras provide some form of connectivity principally to enable recordings to be replayed on a television, or copied to another tape. For our purposes there is only one connector that matters and, fortunately it's one that has been adopted by all digital camera manufacturers. It provides the capability to forge the essential link between camera and computer.

Though universally fitted, FireWire is not allowed the same functionality in all cameras. Some cameras provide only a digital signal *out* capability. This is fine for sending data from the camera to the computer (for editing) but makes the return trip – to the camera for re-recording – impossible. Why would you want to record *back* to the camera? Because once you've edited your production, you want to save the results back to the finest medium available (and one that will permit you to edit again, if you so wish). And that's DV tape.

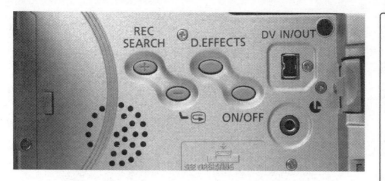

DV sockets are essential for getting digital video recordings out from the camera

The reason for this anomaly is political rather than technical. With a digital input the camcorder is classed (in the EU) as a video recorder and, as such, attracts a small but significant tax surcharge. Hence by disabling this feature manufacturers can circumvent the surcharge and the cameras can be imported at the most economic price.

If you already own such a camera or are seriously thinking about buying one, don't despair. 'Widgets' (that's the name they are sold under!) have been devised by third parties that re-enable the digital input and are available for many of the neutered cameras. There's nothing illegal in this and it's often an expedient way of enabling DV recordings to be made – just be aware that, if you choose this solution, you might compromise the warranty on your camera.

More expensive cameras rarely have this restriction; in the rarefied price bands they inhabit price is less of an issue and the surcharge a less significant component of the final price. FireWire video-in is virtually the norm with all these cameras.

Often overlooked on digital cameras are the conventional, analogue connections. These are still useful to replay your tapes (either as 'raw' footage or edited highlights) on a television or monitor. Look out for *Analogue-in* connectors. These rare beasts will let you record old, analogue footage onto DV tape. It opens up the possibility of converting all your old videotapes (no matter what the original format) to DV and editing these too.

analogue connections are essential for direct replay of video footage

Control-L or Lanc connectors, conversely, are of no use at all for digital editing; these only enable control of the camera by earlier, analogue editing systems.

Data recording

How many wedding videos have you seen that have a crude date and time stamp indelibly recorded in the corner? Though it reminds us of the date (presuming the clock has been correctly configured) the result is quite incongruous and intrusive. It is, for the more enthusiastic video photographer, a sign of poor practice.

With digital video there's no need for the on-screen graphic. When the DV recording format was being devised the fundamental specification featured the requirement to include the automatic recording of record time and date information invisibly at all times. Now with any DV recording you can choose to display it – or hide it - at will. And this embedded data is robust enough to survive editing: you can recall the data at will even if the original material has been through several edits. An important part of this data recording – the timecode – is used in video editing and helps us make precise edits.

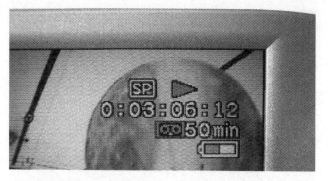

important data can be displayed on screen as well as being recorded invisibly on tape

Manual control

The dedicated video enthusiast, like the professional user, will want complete control over the camera. He or she will want to determine exposure settings, focus control and colour balances. Precise control of these gives far better results than the automatic settings chosen by the camera. But manual filming involves a degree of skill that is not immediately acquired. It is also more time consuming. Camcorders are touted as offering point-and-shoot facilities. Work under manual control and you limit this ability, but ultimately get better video.

Manual overrides are great to have but, if you are happy to permit your camera to make the majority of decisions (which, in virtually all contemporary models, are handled very well) you can make movies successfully without them. The best advice, if you have manual controls, is to keep the camera in 'auto' as a matter of course. Then you are prepared for that once in a lifetime shot. Switch to manual when you have the time to exploit the power.

Faders and special effects

In-camera effects, of which fades and other special effects are examples, are largely superfluous if you intend to edit your movies later. The same effects (and often a lot more) can be introduced thanks to the editing software. At this stage you'll have much more control over the way each effect is implemented. So, when you're at the viewfinder concentrate on gathering footage and nothing else. Remember if you apply your effects in-camera you can't remove or change it later!

in-camera special effects have no place in digital video production

You'll find some cameras now allow in-camera editing. This is ideal for someone who doesn't want the trouble of desktop editing, but the editing facilities are severely limited and no match for even the most rudimentary desktop system. Again, for desktop editing this is a superfluous feature and should have no place on your 'wish' list.

Still camera mode

Many digital video cameras have the ability to record still images. Press a button (usually marked 'snapshot') and a still image is recorded normally on to a small, removable memory card in the camera. These still images can then be copied to a computer either via a connection to the camera or by placing the memory card in a reader attached to the computer, in the same manner as you might for the memory cards used with digital still cameras.

The nature of the imaging chip and recording system of the camera means that quality is mediocre by still camera standards but with resolutions of up to 1200 × 900 pixels possible on some top models acceptable print quality can be achieved.

The effective film speed of cameras

Most people who take up video – digital or otherwise – have had some experience of conventional photography and tend to be reasonably familiar with the film speed, the measure of the sensitivity of film emulsion. But how does this equate with the sensitivity of a camera's CCD? Digital stills cameras often have settings calibrated in effective film speeds (measured in ISO) but video cameras use the *Lux* measurement. Precise comparisons are impossible and (in all but the most exacting situations) irrelevant, but Table 3 shows how Lux and ISO (sensitivity) figures compare for an aperture of F11. This is, for example the setting you would use on an exposure meter when using this to set a video camera manually.

Table 3

Film Speed (ISO)	Film Type	Lux
50	'slow'	4000
100	'average'	2000
400	'Universal'	500
800	'fast'	250

Bluetooth and the Internet

The much-touted Bluetooth technology enables compatible devices to be linked without any physical connection. In the digital video world this communications technology enables cameras and mobile phones to communicate and for movies (or still images) to be emailed immediately after recording. To make use of Bluetooth you'll need an appropriate camera and mobile phone. You'll also have to record your movie in a format that can be emailed. As conventional digital video generates enormous files – usually measured in hundreds of megabytes – this is obviously unsuitable for sending; instead you'll need to record in the more compact MPEG1 format. Few cameras offer MPEG1 recording but if this feature could be important to you, ensure that you audition appropriate models

The best time to buy?

The inevitable question many buyers will ask is 'Is now a good time to buy?' This question is no doubt triggered by the knowledge (gleaned from magazines or rumours from the Web) of there being something even better than your intended purchase, just around the corner. Unfortunately, no matter when you buy there will be something that bit better waiting in the wings. It's how the manufacturers of such cameras make their money, enticing us to upgrade periodically.

But to hesitate now will mean you might miss something more precious, like your children growing up, that once in a lifetime trip or a unique business opportunity. Think of your camera as nothing more than a tool: it's simply letting you gather memories and imagery.

The future

So what of the future for digital video? We'll undoubtedly see an increase in disc-based (or even solid-state) recording media both of which offer more flexible and durable recording. Cameras featuring solid-state memory for storage have already appeared, although given the quantity of information that needs to be stored and the (comparatively) high price of memory chips, such cameras tend to offer low quality video and have short recording times.

What you can be sure of is that whatever the format of the future, your current digital material will be easy to use alongside material in that new format.

Summary

Whether buying for the first time or upgrading here are the main points to bear in mind, particularly if you intend to edit your movies.

- Does it have the right connections? A FireWire out connection is a must, FireWire in is highly recommended.
- Is size important? If so, look at the small, pocketable models. Otherwise the palm-sized models (which are often a little cheaper) may be more appropriate.
- Do you have a collection of Video8 or Hi-8 tapes? Consider a Digital8 camera. The limited range on offer will be offset by the backwards compatibility.
- In any model look for a good lens. Don't base your decision on the 'power' of the digital zoom.
- Check the viewfinders. If you'll be videoing outside much of the time is the LCD panel up to the job?

- Do you *need* manual control? If you do, make sure your camera has all the controls you need and that they are easy to use. If not, some manual control may be a bonus.
- Special effects, still camera mode and *title generators* are largely superfluous to the digital video editor. Your camera will inevitably come with some; just don't bother using them!
- Do you need to create email video or email video footage from a location (such as from holiday or your business site)? Investigate Bluetooth compatible models.

04

the first download

In this chapter you will learn:
- how to download video to your computer
- how to transfer material from old video tape
- about replaying your downloaded video.

It may seem inverse logic to discuss the downloading (and in the following chapters, the manipulation) of video recordings when we haven't as yet investigated the *making* of those recordings but there's a good reason for this. By understanding the processes of acquiring raw movie footage and compiling that into something more meaningful we are better able to understand what we need to record. This will give us the opportunity, later, to craft our video photography techniques to the needs of desktop editing.

In this chapter we'll look at the preparations we need to make to our computer, prior to downloading. We'll ensure that the software we intend to use is best configured to accept the footage and the computer itself is fully optimized. In making the connection we'll investigate how easy – or how difficult – this process actually is and, in particular, the perils and pitfalls.

Preparing to download

Preparing to download your digital video from your camera to the computer is straightforward. You'll need your chosen video editing software loaded, a FireWire board or connector installed (or provided via an external module) and the appropriate FireWire cable. Of course you'll also need your camera loaded with a tape containing the footage you'd like to download.

Computer preparations

The computer itself needs little preparation *per se*, assuming that it conforms to the 'typical' specifications we outlined in Chapter 2 or those recommended by the software manufacturer.

Hard disc space is a vital resource to digital video downloads, and you need to adjust your thinking to file sizes measured in gigabytes rather than kilobytes or megabytes! As a good rule of thumb, using the DV format, five minutes of video recording will consume one gigabyte. It's a good idea to budget for all the material you need and about 25 per cent more though some editing processes may require the provision of additional space.

Here's a ready reckoner for hard disc space required for your video (Table 4).

Table 4

Video duration	Required hard disc space
1 second	4 MB
1 minute	230 MB
10 minutes	2 GB
30 minutes	6 GB
1 hour	12 GB

These figures are based on the capture of DV format video. Other formats (such as the MPEG2 or Sony's MicroMV, or the selectable lower resolutions possible with some software) will consume less.

Starting your software

When starting your video editing software for the first time you may be prompted to enter the name of a project. This will be the project name for your movie and will also be the name given to the folder in which all the video clips, when downloaded, are stored. Any other media, such as sound files and still images, will also be kept here.

When you start the software on subsequent sessions you will (depending on the application) automatically be taken to the last project you were working on. The number of concurrent projects you can have may again depend on the application or, more likely, be limited by the amount of disc space available to store the relevant resources.

when launching the software you can specify a new project or select an existing one

Making the connection

We mentioned earlier that if your computer does not feature a FireWire connection but is otherwise appropriately specified for handling digital video, that FireWire cards can be purchased and fitted internally. If you are using a laptop you can use a FireWire adaptor that plugs into your PC Card (PCMCIA) port.

The beauty of FireWire is that it is a standard, so we need have no undue worries about compatibility. However, that standard is stretched a little when it comes to the connecting cable. Connections on cameras are invariably of the four-pin variety; those on computers generally six pin. Hence you'll need a four-pin to six-pin FireWire cable to make the link between the two. We say *generally* as some computers (particularly Windows laptops) use connectors that are also four pin, requiring a four-pin to four-pin cable. Sometimes you'll find an appropriate cable has been provided with the camera (or even the FireWire card, if an accessory card has been used). If not you can purchase one from most computer and photo stores. One- and two-metre lengths are normally offered; the longer one is a better buy as it offers more flexibility in placement.

Why are there four- and six-pin connections? The FireWire standard permits the power to some external devices to be delivered by the connection and this power supply system accounts for the two extra connections. A camcorder requires more power than the computer can supply and will rely on its own resources, hence it has a four-pin connection; with deference to their limited battery power and more modest power supply, laptops don't generally offer powered FireWire (though all Apple laptops offer six-pin connections).

the typical FireWire cable has a six-pin connection at the computer end and four-pin for the camera

A successful connection

Many manufacturers, whether of computers, video cameras or software, will tell you how easy their product makes the process of downloading video recordings to the computer hard disc. There will be descriptions of systems working in perfect harmony . . . but is this actually the case, and what contingencies do we need to make or at least be aware of?

Making the physical connection is simple. Connect the FireWire cable to the camera and then to the computer. Often, for protection, the FireWire connection will be concealed under a rubberized flap or door along with other connections. You may see it indicated by the FireWire symbol, the i.Link symbol (in the case of Sony cameras) or simply 'DV in/out'. Your camcorder has two modes: Record and Playback (these may be labelled with slightly different but equivalent terms such as Record and VCR or Movie and VTR). You'll need to select Playback – the same mode you use when viewing your recordings.

When the camera is turned on the computer will recognize the device and advise you accordingly. If you have an appropriate video editing package running you will see the message 'Camera Connected' or similar.

It is a good idea to use your camera's mains adaptor, rather than battery, when connected to the computer. This way you'll prevent any possible problem due to a power failure during the download.

Connection problems

If the computer doesn't recognize the device or acknowledge that it is connected, some quick diagnostics should isolate (and hopefully address) the problem.

- First check the camera is turned on. It sounds obvious, but it is easy to overlook. Some cameras can 'time out' or sleep after a few minutes' inactivity. Also check that you have selected Playback mode on the camera.

- Check that the cables are properly connected. FireWire cable connections are simple push-fit types and not locking. It is possible for them to work loose, particularly if either the camera or computer is moved.

- Be aware of any special requirements with regard to turning on the camera and starting the software. Some software is particular about whether the camera or software is started first – check your software manual's Getting Started pages.

- Check that the software drivers for your camera are installed. The drivers ensure compatibility between the application and the device. Though most cameras are supported by most software there will be occasions when (perhaps because your camera is a new or unusual model) you'll need to source a specific driver. Refer to the camcorder's manual in the first instance, and then the websites of the manufacturers of camera and software.

- If you still have no joy the problem may be in the FireWire cable or connection. If you can, test the FireWire ports with another device (such as a compatible CD writer or scanner) and examine the cable. If you have another, substitute it. If you have had a FireWire card added, ensure that it was fitted correctly (return to the dealer who fitted it and have them check it out).

Only if all these steps fail will you need to refer your computer to the dealer. In practice you'll find few compatibility problems and most that do occur are addressed above.

The first transfer

It's time to test those connections and the efficacy of your chosen software application by undertaking a real video transfer.

Start up your video editing software and turn on the video camera. If you haven't already, insert a pre-recorded tape.

If this is your first video transfer you may have concerns that you could damage or otherwise compromise your precious video footage. Be assured that your original material is quite safe. Although we talk extensively about 'downloading' or 'transferring' video footage we actually mean copying. The footage that makes its way to our hard disc is merely a copy of the original; that original on our tape remains unaffected by the process. For additional reassurance every digital videocassette features a safety switch that prevents the erasure of the tape which can be switched to the 'save' position. It is a good idea to use this switch on any recorded tape to prevent unintentional reuse.

all cassettes feature a tab that can be slid between save and record (shown here) positions

Check the 'Camera Connected' message has appeared (as here with iMovie).

0:08:23:11

Camera Connected

Now the software has effectively taken control of the camera and the on-screen tape controls (below the main picture window) can be used to play, wind and rewind the tape. Take a few moments to play with these controls, and watch the video being replayed in the window.

You may be surprised that the quality of the video shown in the window is not equivalent to that you might see on the camera's LCD panel and is certainly inferior to that you'd expect to see during replay on a television or monitor. Don't worry. Though the picture may not be the best, be assured that the quality of the video being copied, and that which you will eventually output, will be up to the excellent DV standard.

a replay screen

Some software will provide options (usually found under the Preferences sub-menu option) to alter the quality of the playback, for example between low quality video with smooth motion, or high quality video with slightly more jerky motion. Given that neither selection will affect the video itself, choose that which makes viewing more comfortable.

Note that you are currently using your computer only to view your video: though your footage is buzzing along your FireWire cable and being replayed through the computer we are not, as yet, copying anything to the hard disc.

To start the data capture wind the tape to your chosen start position and press the Import button. The camera will start up, the video will play in the window and your video clips will start loading. In the case of iMovie, thumbnails representing the first frame of each clip appear on the 'shelf' to the right of the main window. These clips correspond to each scene in the movie. The software identifies the start and finish of each scene.

each scene is identified sequentially
numbers refer to duration in seconds

A useful indicator, seen here below the shelf, shows the remaining available hard disc space.

Free Space: 3.83GB

free disc space indicator

When the video has finished downloading, you can stop the import (click on the Import button in this case). You can now review any of the video clips you have imported by clicking on the thumbnail on the shelf. The selected clip appears in the window and can be replayed by using the conventional VCR-type controls. For a more precise examination of the video you can move the pointer (known as the playhead) along the scrubber bar beneath the window that represents the time axis of the video.

scrubber bar

That's it! Your first batch of digital video has been downloaded. It has now been copied as a series of clips to the project folder on the hard disc.

Transferring video from an analogue source

Though this book is about digital video, there may be occasions when you will want or need to transfer video that has been recorded using analogue equipment.

Overall, the process of transferring analogue video is similar to digital, except that you will be using an analogue to digital converter box (such as the Formac Studio or Dazzle's Hollywood DV Bridge, both of which we mentioned earlier) or an equivalent converter mounted within the computer.

External converter boxes behave, so far as the computer software is concerned, as digital video cameras and are generally connected via a FireWire cable in the same way. You may even get the same 'Camera Connected' message when the converter is turned on. Both iMovie and VideoWave recognize converters in this way. Windows users may have to connect the audio output of the converter box to the line-in connection on the computer as audio signals are sometimes not carried on the FireWire. Though your converter box will be recognized as a digital camera you won't be able to use the import button in the software in the same way. You will have to start the tape on the connected analogue camcorder (or video recorder deck) manually, pressing the Import button to start data transfer at the appropriate point.

A–D converters require a connection to the analogue equipment on one side and the computer on the other
alternate connectors are often provided

Scene breaks

Much of the ease of importing digital video is due to the automatic splitting of the video into clips, based on the 'hidden' data recorded alongside the video and audio. Some applications (including iMovie) are able to detect scene changes based on the abrupt change to the video signal at each transition and can thus split the digitized data into clips. Other applications also include this feature, though not necessarily as an automatic one. If yours doesn't (or you can't find out how to enable it) don't worry. We will soon discover how to split a video manually into separate clips.

Reviewing the downloaded video

The downloading process has probably been unremarkable. Each scene from your video will have been recorded on the computer and a small thumbnail image from the start of each is now shown. Now you need to review one or all of these to ensure that the process has been successful. In doing so we'll be replaying the copy of the video that is on the computer's hard disc.

Click on any of the thumbnails and the start of the corresponding scene will appear in the main window. Use the control buttons to play, wind and rewind your video as you would the corresponding controls on a conventional videocassette recorder. Unlike the original tape-based copy you can move around the video at will, with no time lost while the tape itself winds or rewinds.

VideoWave
preview
screen

Digital video really pushes your computer to the limit. You are asking it to do an immense amount of processing and, in general, it will acquit itself well. However, because the video processing is being done 'live', should your computer be side-tracked by another program or application that is running there is a chance of losing the odd frame that should have been recorded during that operation. The result when the video is replayed is an occasional jump or stutter that, although brief, is sufficient to make viewing uncomfortable.

Avoiding the problem involves minimizing the number of other programs running concurrently with your application and managing a few housekeeping duties. Follow these simple precautions to make your video footage glitch-free:

• Close all other applications prior to running your video editing software. This prevents the computer allocating them time and resources (even if you are not actively using them at the same time as your video editor).

• Temporarily switch off any screensavers or virus scanners as these make demands (both periodic and continuous) on your computer resources.

• Keep your hard disc tidy. Run a disc defragmentation program (such as Windows Disk Defragmenter) to keep the free space on your hard disc contiguous. This prevents the computer losing time 'hunting' for free space.

• Switch off any other background processes. Any program that runs periodically will cause some interruption.

• Don't use Virtual Memory. Virtual memory is an ideal way of making a greater amount of RAM memory available to most programs and processes through the allocation of an area of the hard disc as virtual RAM. Unfortunately transferring data to and from virtual memory takes much longer than RAM, again resulting in interrupts.

• Run Disk Cleanup (Windows) to remove any temporary files.

Even with all these precautions you may still get the odd dropped frame but now they will be less significant and less distracting. Professional software often includes a feature for 'smoothing over' dropped frames, making them invisible. Having a second hard disc – dedicated to video captures – is another way to reduce dropped frames. It is a more expensive solution but one that many video enthusiasts have turned to because it also offers the opportunity to install a much larger hard drive.

editing basics

In this chapter you will learn:
- the first steps in video editing
- how to assemble video clips into a movie
- about linking scenes.

Editing is the pivotal process where our raw footage is transformed into a movie. Though digital video editing on the PC is a unique process the fundamental basis and much of the terminology hail from the traditional movie editing business.

Consider, for a moment, the onerous task of the professional movie editor. He or she will have been given hundreds of real film clips representing scenes from the movie along with the script and storyline. Rack after rack of celluloid will then need to be examined before even an approximate sequence can be considered. As it is quite common to film scenes out of sequence it becomes the responsibility of the editor to navigate this massive collection of clips and realize the director's vision. It is little wonder, then, that a movie that has taken six weeks to film may take ten times as long to edit.

Of course, our productions will be on a more modest scale. And in most cases our combined roles of cameraman, director and editor work mostly in our favour and only occasionally against.

But in our role as editor we have the benefit of technology that makes the process, at least from a technical standpoint, very simple. We've just seen how easy it is to capture data. Let's now see how easy editing is too.

For our first attempts we won't do anything too ambitious. We'll learn how to convert the raw footage we acquired into more meaningful – and useable – material. We'll see how easy it is to manipulate digital clips, cutting, trimming and joining them. We'll then look more closely at the way we link clips together and in particular how to use special techniques known as transitions to make joins less abrupt and more meaningful.

The first edit

Assuming that we have acquired it from a digital source (or used software that detects scene changes) the footage that now resides on our computer hard disc has been divided neatly into individual clips. Apart from being divided these clips are a direct copy of the original material. And that original material undoubtably contains, among others, over-long scenes, alternate scenes, bad shots and that interminably long scene taken when you forgot to press the 'pause' button.

For our first step we need to trim footage that is unsuitable or inappropriate. By ruthlessly discarding material that is obviously flawed we are able to concentrate our attentions on the good. We can remove redundant footage in two ways.

The first is to ignore it. While the clips are collected on our shelf (the iMovie term) or library (VideoWave) they are not contributing to the movie and unless we use them they will be ignored. This is a somewhat untidy approach. If something is of no value why keep it? And given that this footage is consuming vast tracts of your hard disc yet serving no useful purpose why keep it?

The more satisfactory option is to remove this material now. Drag the unwanted clips to the Trash bin and delete them. Should you find that you really do need a deleted scene then remember that the original is still on your tape. You can easily retrieve it later should the need arise. Let's now look at some very simple processes that enable us to cut our clips into shape. In particular we'll investigate the use of the split and trim commands.

Splitting clips

Often, though, the redundant material is part of a clip that also contains material that we wish to retain. With superfluous material at the start or finish, say, we first need to split the clip so that the unwanted parts can be discarded.

There are more reasons why we may want to split a clip into two or more pieces. We may have an inordinately long scene that we wish to divide into two or more meaningful pieces. We may have a digitized analogue recording in which there are no scene breaks. We might even have a long piece of video recorded from an analogue source that has not been successfully divided into individual scenes.

The process of splitting a clip is straightforward. Here's how you would split a clip containing two scenes at the scene boundary using iMovie and VideoWave. Remember that though these instructions are specific to these applications they are very similar to those that would be employed to achieve the same with other packages.

iMovie
In iMovie we need not worry about splitting a clip at a scene boundary – every scene will, without fail, be split at the appropriate boundary. With iMovie we need worry about

splitting only if the scene we have is too long or contains superfluous material that we need to hive off.

1 Begin by selecting your clip (click or double click on the clip's thumbnail) so that it appears in the main window.

2 Play the clip so that you are familiar with its contents and aware of the position of the playhead corresponding to the splitting position.

3 Move the playhead using the mouse so that it is precisely positioned along the scrubber bar at the scene change point.

playhead

4 Split the clip using the menu command Edit menu ‡ Split Clip at playhead (or use the shortcut key combination of Command+T).

5 Your clip will be split and both new clips will appear on the shelf. The suffixes /1 and /2 have been added to the clip names to distinguish each.

It is a good idea to play each clip after splitting to confirm that the division has taken place at the correct point. Unless you were spot on there's a chance that a frame or two from one scene could be attached to the other. If this is the case we can deal with it by trimming (see below).

VideoWave

VideoWave offers a scene change detection feature for splitting your video into clips in the same manner as iMovie. However, this feature can be slightly idiosyncratic and works best only after a degree of fine tuning. This can be a somewhat fiddly process and it is often faster to use the Scene Detection dialogue box.

1 Before capturing video ensure that the Run Scene Detection on Captured Video check box is ticked (click on it if necessary). You'll find this box on the Start Capture panel.

2 Capture your video. Note that scene detection does not occur live as the video is acquired.
3 Afterwards an options panel will appear. Select Manual.
4 Move the playhead triangle to the point on the timeline that represents the start of the scene.
5 Click on Manually Add Scene. The scene will be added to the library and indicated by a thumbnail of the first frame. If you wish, you can rename your scene to make it something more memorable.

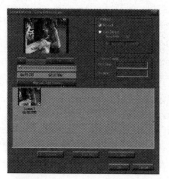

6 Repeat for subsequent scenes.

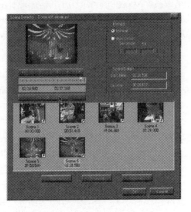

As we mentioned with regard to scene splitting in iMovie it is a good idea to review each of the scenes after they have been split to ensure that the split has occurred at precisely the right point. It is very easy for a single frame from the next or preceeding scene to be attached to the current. Although it will only be on screen for one-twenty-fifth of a second, it will be enough for your audience to notice!

Trimming clips

Trimming is a similar processes to splitting, though this time the superfluous material is discarded rather than being retained as a 'new' clip. Here are the ways to trim a clip in iMovie and VideoWave.

iMovie

iMovie gives three ways of performing a trim based on whether there is material to be removed at both ends of the clip, at one end or in the middle.

In the case of superfluous material at each end we can use the Crop command. According to Apple this is the 'official' way of trimming. It is certainly the most thorough, though not the most expedient in all cases.

1 Click the clip to select it and display it in the monitor window.
2 Click below the scrubber bar and move the playhead triangles to the start of the material you wish to keep. Two triangles appear on the indexed line below the scrubber bar.

3 Drag the rightmost handle along the scrubber bar to the end of the area you wish to keep (so that footage to be discarded is to the right). You will scroll through the movie clip as you drag the triangle 'handle'. The scrubber bar darkens to show the material that is to be retained.

4 Choose Crop from the Edit menu. The markers and the darkened area on the scrubber bar will disappear to indicate that the clip has been trimmed according to your instructions.

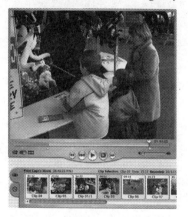

5 The trimmed elements have been sent to the Trash (note that the capacity of the Trash has increased). If you have made a mistake, or want to alter the crop you can use the Undo command to restore the trimmed parts and retrieve them from the trash.

To trim material from one end of the clip you would use the Split Clip at Playhead command after first positioning the playhead then discarding the unwanted clip. Or we could use the triangle handles that we used to Crop the scene.

1 Click the clip to select it and display it in the monitor window.

2 Click below the scrubber bar to make the triangles appear and move these to the boundary of the material to be kept and that to be removed. Drag the appropriate handle (depending on whether the material to be removed is at the

start or finish) to select the footage to be discarded. As before, the scrubber bar will darken to show the selected footage.

3 Select Cut from the Edit menu.
4 This time the selected footage is removed and sent to the Trash bin.

Note that, as in word processing applications, Cut takes the removed material and pastes it into the clipboard. You can then use the paste command (Edit menu → Paste) to paste the clip elsewhere. Hence you could use this method to split a clip, pasting the removed piece back on the shelf.

Removing footage from the middle of a clip (i.e. retaining footage either side) doesn't sound a very credible 'real world' situation but does come into its own when working with extended clips where intermediate material can be removed, perhaps to insert other scenes.

1 Click the clip to select it and display it in the monitor window.
2 Click below the scrubber bar to make the handles appear and position these to define the limits of the footage to be removed.

3 Select Edit → Cut.

The material left behind now comprises two clips. A new clip (containing the footage from after the trimmed area) has been created and placed next to the original. That original now comprises the footage from before the trimmed section. The two clips will be clearly identified. If the original clip was 'Scene 23' the adjacent newcomer will be 'Scene 23/1'.

VideoWave

Clips can be trimmed in VideoWave's Cutting Room using a method that is similar to that used by professional editing systems. You will use the playhead to define 'In' and 'Out' positions. The 'In' position describes the new start point and the 'Out' the end point.

1 Click on a clip to select it and display it in the monitor window.

2 Click on the Cutting Room icon to open the Cutting Room controls.

3 Move the playhead (the light triangle) to the start point of your chosen footage and click on the Mark In Time button (to the bottom left of the control panel below the monitor window).

4 Move the playhead to the point of the end of your selection and click on the Mark Out Time button.

5 Click Apply to enact the trim. Depending on the length of the clip and the size of the trim the monitor may clear and the message Generating Preview appear for a few seconds.

Assembling clips

After trimming and splitting our collection of clips and discarding unwanted material we will be left with those clips that we'll want to use to assemble our movie. We can now assemble the clips into a finished movie. We are more concerned at this stage to assess whether the clips will run together successfully. We can later refine the edit to make a more successful compilation.

Whether our movie is to tell a story or be a record of an event, say, there is no 'right' way to build it. Putting the clips together roughly in a sequence or rough cut like this enables us to try different clip ordering and helps us assess any further editing that might be required. By compiling this rough cut we can check whether scenes are correctly sequenced with regard to the intended storyline.

To create a sequence using either iMovie or VideoWave all we need to do is select a clip and drag it to the timeline. In fact, both products use a simple filmstrip-like timeline that is better described as a storyboard. As subsequent clips are dropped on the storyboard they will be linked to the preceding one. If we wish a particular clip to be placed between two others then we can drop it in the gap and the following clips will be repositioned automatically.

Storyboards and timelines

What is the difference between a storyboard and a timeline? Principally it is one of the representation of clips. A timeline is a very literal representation of the movie with the axis calibrated in units of time (usually seconds, but optionally minutes where a more condensed view is required). A short clip will be represented by a short block along the timeline, a long clip by a correspondingly longer one. Parallel tracks show audio tracks with a similar representation.

Storyboards, conversely, show only a thumbnail for each clip no matter how long. Usefully iMovie gives us the option of displaying our sequence as either a storyboard (the default setting) or a timeline. Clicking on the tabs (one marked with an eye icon to denote the storyboard layout, the other a clockface for the timeline) to the left of the display switches from one to the other.

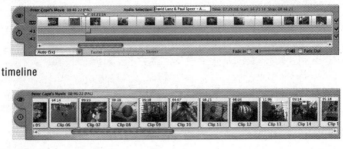

timeline

storyboard

Telling a story

It is a good idea to spend a little time reviewing the available clips before beginning to compile a sequence. Even if there is no obvious story to your production there will still be a logical flow of events which needs to be considered. The beauty of editing in this way is that all clips are immediately at hand. You can build a movie using any sequence of clips in the firm knowledge that if the results are inappropriate or not to your liking you can alter the sequence at will. Any assembly of clips on the timeline or storyboard can be played or replayed at will.

Linking scenes

Once we've dropped some or all of our clips on to the timeline we need to consider how they should be linked. Currently, as with the original movie, there is a simple 'cut' between scenes. If we examined them frame by frame we would see that the final frame of one scene would be followed by the first frame of the next. Digital video editing gives us the opportunity to add transitional effects (usually called simply transitions) between scenes. Transitions – such as one scene fading in, while the previous fades out – can improve the flow of your production and add to the interest.

VideoWave illustrates transitions pictorially

If you watch closely you'll see that transitions are used extensively in film and television productions. Follow the lead of the professional and examine how they are used. For most productions a simple jump cut (i.e. no transition effect) is quite sufficient and for others a cross fade of one scene into the next makes an elegant transition. At the start and end (and possibly where commercial breaks might have been intended) they will add a fade in or out.

The more complex and startling effects tend to be used more sparingly as they can, if used frequently, irritate the viewing audience. It is often said that the best transition is that which the viewer does not notice.

Both iMovie and VideoWave include a set of transitions that are easily applied.

Applying transitions in iMovie

A transition is easily added between any two clips.

1 Click on the Transitions tab below iMovie's clip shelf to open the Transitions palette.

2 Select a transition. Your selection will be previewed in the Preview window.

3 For directional transitions (where the new image moves up, down or across the original) specify a direction using the four-way button adjacent to the menu.

4 Adjust the speed of the transition.

5 Drag and drop the transition name (or the preview) to the gap between the intended clips on the timeline. The transition will automatically be inserted and the rendering will begin.

Note that the duration of the clips and the transition must be 'compatible'. This means that nominally a transition should never be longer than half the length of the clip to which it is applied and usually should be somewhat less. The software will prevent an inappropriately timed transition from being applied. Using either the Storyboard or Timeline representations, the transition is shown.

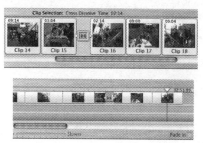

Applying transitions in VideoWave

1 Click on the gap between the two clips where you wish to apply the transition.

2 Select the Transitions room from the Mode Selector.

3 Choose a transition. By running your mouse over each of the thumbnails you'll get a preview of how each transition works.

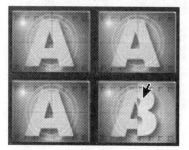

4 Alter the transition duration by using the + and − buttons.
5 Click the Apply button to apply the transition. A corresponding icon will appear in the transition space.

You can also find additional transitional effects (usually those of a more bizarre variety) available from online sources, often as freeware or shareware.

Summary

We've now converted our footage into an embryonic movie. Superfluous material has been removed and the story is now 'tighter'. Transitions have altered the pace of the movie, making scene changes less abrupt and more flowing. If we now take the time to review our movie we will begin to see how originally disjointed scenes have now been woven into a story. Okay, so it will not be perfect and some crucial elements have so far been neglected. Some of these we'll investigate over the next two chapters when we explore the addition of special effects and titles and then sound.

titles and special effects

In this chapter you will learn:
- how to add titles
- about creating titles on location and your desktop
- about special effects.

Special effects can make or break a movie. Used with care and deference they can add to the power and impact. Used haphazardly and without care or due attention they will make your movie memorable – for all the wrong reasons. Likewise, titles can be an important embellishment or needless distraction. Let's begin by looking at the options for title creation.

Titles

There is no reason why your movie should contain any titles at all. Many producers argue that if you have crafted your story with care the storyline should be clear enough to obviate the need. In practice, however, there are several reasons why titles (a general term that we use to cover titles, captions and credits) are useful.

Some of these reasons are:
• to give a 'finished' effect to the production
• to help explain situations or events that are not immediately obvious
• to help divide a production into 'visual chapters'
• not least, to provide the opportunity to promote yourself in the credits.

The key to the use of titles is to make them meaningful. Throwing titles in for the hell of it will be distracting and can patronise viewers. Short, Simple, Bold is the mantra when creating titles:

• Short: A short succinct title is more effective than a long one and is easier to read.

- Simple: Conventional fonts are easiest to read; don't make your audience squint at an unusual font.

- Bold: Keep the text size moderately large. Very large text may look absurd but small text will be difficult to read.

Of course there will be circumstances when rules like these need to be broken. By all means do so but ensure that your titles 'work' not only when you view them on your computer monitor but also when they are transferred back to video, say, and played back on a television. And if you are planning to output the movie in alternate versions – such as a heavily compressed version for emailing – the reduced quality may make further demands on the type of text used. Serif fonts, like Times, may look fine on a television but are likely to become difficult to read on a compressed video. A san-serif font such as Arial is more effective here. If you plan to use streamed video (p.150) text can look very poor indeed, even when you take the precaution of large, bold characters. In this case it is better to avoid text altogether.

The font is an important consideration because it can also imply the type of movie that follows. Times is a formal font and is best used with formal productions such as traditional weddings and 'serious' documentary. A softer, informal font like Comic Sans is more appropriate to children's parties.

Times New Roman

Arial (sans serif)

Arial Rounded

Comic Sans

Think too about colour. Because we often have the option of using any colour from the extensive colour palette we sometimes try to use something extreme – just to be different. Strong colours rarely work. They are harder on the eye and many shades cannot be reproduced accurately (or with the same degree of saturation) on television screens. The result is either a more mediocre shade or a bright intense colour that smears into the surrounding image.

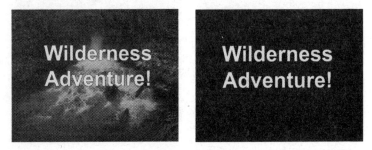

It is best to stick to one colour throughout and if this is white or a pale, off white you'll find it will work equally well whether you choose to show it against a black background or superimposed over video footage (unless, of course, you're making a video about a skiing holiday ...).

Creating titles on location

Titles are often left until the video editing stage when the software can be invoked to apply the appropriate text. But more effective titles can often be produced on location, as you record your original raw footage.

The source of such titling is manyfold. It could be signage – a beach sign for example, to introduce a beach movie – or perhaps some relevant ephemera pertinent to the event. A good example of this is to use a wedding invitation as the main title for a wedding video, or a close-up of a rail or air ticket for a travel video. Such titles need a little more thought but can produce an ultimately more satisfying result. Your audience will certainly welcome your efforts.

And some titles need not contain words at all! For example, the 'title' for a movie about a day trip to London might consist of an opening shot showing some landmarks cross fading into each other.

You could replace a title altogether and use a short narrative introduction. If you find that you are unable to produce a short, snappy title then this may be an ideal alternative. We'll look more at the practicalities of adding sound a little later.

Don't, on any account, use the camcorder's own titling feature. The good news is that, though once common, thankfully very few camcorders now include one of these. These devices – which add crude, block text over the recorded footage – had their day when there was little opportunity to post-produce your video but their overtly crude nature is not appropriate for the more sophisticated marketplace today. Also, such superimposed titles were permanently burned into the recording. So, were you to decide later that it was inappropriate, mis-spelt or unreadable you would have been out of luck. There was no way of going back to the original footage. No. If your camera features a title option, leave it well alone.

Creating titles using video editing software

All video editing applications provide the option of adding titles and often feature a wide range of layouts. You'll have the ability to add conventional titles and other text such as rolling credits and even subtitles.

It is usual to have the option of creating the title as 'new' footage by superimposing text over a plain (usually black) background. This can be effective at separating the titles from the video production itself; it also focuses the viewer's attention on the text rather than competing with video images. Alternatively the title can be superimposed over a still image, which may be a still shot from video footage or specially created (for example using a digital still camera).

Titles using iMovie

Pressing the Titles tab beneath the shelf reveals iMovie's titling tools. Then adding a title involves these six steps:

1 Selecting a title effect type.
2 Choosing a text font.
3 Typing the text.
4 Setting the duration of the title.
5 Selecting a text colour.
6 Adding a backdrop.

Depending on the type of title and the effect you desire you can also specify a direction (for rolling credits, for example) and choose a black background.

Here's a little more detail on each.

1 Selecting a title effect type: The central scroll menu includes a list of title types including the plain 'Centered Title' [sic] through various animated types ('Flying Words', 'Scrolling

Block' and 'Rolling Credits') to more specialized ('Subtitle', 'Stripe Subtitle' and 'Zoom'). Although the default set provided is sufficient to meet most eventualities, there are further options that can be downloaded from Apple's iMovie website (www.apple.com/imovie). When you select a type an example (based on the currently selected font and font size) will be displayed in the Preview window. If your have selected an animated menu, the animation will be demonstrated.

2 Choosing a text font: The default font is Times but you can select any alternative from those revealed by clicking on the Menu button. Note that if you have an extensive font collection on your computer not all of them will necessarily be displayed; only TrueType fonts can be used. Non-TrueType fonts won't be shown. If you have distributed documents to other computer users you'll be aware that sometimes they do not reproduce in the same way on those computers. This is because those computers may not have the same font set and will be unable to reproduce that which you used. Don't worry about this happening with your video – the titles will be imprinted into the video. You can alter the size of the text by using the slider bar. The relative size is displayed on the preview screen.

3 Typing the text: By default the text box will read 'My Great Movie' along with your name. Unless you intend this to be your title, you'll need to type in the new text. Simply highlight the current text (by clicking in the appropriate box) and type in your replacement. The type of text box will depend upon the title type you have selected. Simple titles feature only two lines, those for credits four. Others, including the 'Music Video' enable a block of text to be pasted in. You'll need to judge for yourself (bearing in mind the points raised above) how much is appropriate or desirable. Note also that when using the smaller text boxes, text in the top line of any pair is usually reproduced in a slightly larger font size than in the bottom.

4 Setting the duration of the title: For each of the title types
there are minimum and maximum durations. Centered
Multiple, for example, has a minimum duration of 1.15
seconds and maximum of 9.15. The slow-building Flying
letters has a more pedestrian minimum and maximum of 4
and 32 seconds respectively. The best way to determine how
long to display your title is to calculate how long it takes to
read through slowly twice. If, like Flying Letters, the title
takes time to build, you'll need to allow longer. You can also
set a pause duration for some title types. The text of scrolling
titles, for example, can be made to pause mid-screen for a
pre-determined time. If the settings seem complex, don't
worry. You can preview your results and test different settings
until you have one that you are comfortable with.

5 Selecting a text colour: Click on the little window above the
Font Selection menu and you'll see a range of colours appear.
You'll see that this palette is somewhat more muted and dull
compared with the normal colour palettes offered in
applications. Using one of these colours will prevent the
problems we discussed earlier and will be more restful for the
viewer.

6 Adding a backdrop: Forget, for a moment, the practicalities
and imagine what backdrop you would like behind your
titles. Black? The opening scene from the movie? A still shot?
Any of these is possible. Selecting black is the easiest: simply
click on the 'Over Black' button. Your title, of appropriate
duration, will be created and can be appended or attached to
your movie by dragging and dropping. Leave this box
unticked and you can apply the title over a selected movie
scene. To use a still image you'll need to import that image
into iMovie (we will go into more detail about the importing
and exporting of still images on p.108). Apple again, via their
website, provide us with a range of Hollywoodesque
backgrounds (satin drapes, spotlight patterns) that can be
downloaded.

The small four-way button next to the Title Type menu can be used to determine the direction in which moving titles will travel. Conventionally credits, for example, will scroll from the bottom to top. Select the down arrow and they will move downwards. Clearly some options, such as this, will be less comfortable to read. Again play with the preview to see if a specific effect or combination works.

The title is added to the movie by dragging the Preview window to the movie track at the appropriate position. Note that if you want the title to be placed in the middle of a clip you will need to split that clip at the insertion point (see p.67, Splitting Clips).

Titles using VideoWave

In VideoWave titles – and text of all types – are produced using the Text Animator feature. Text Animator is selected from the Mode Selector bar.

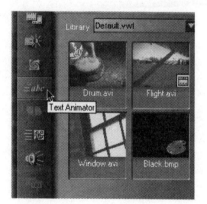

Creating a title in VideoWave involves:

1 Selecting an animation style.
2 Entering the title type.
3 Selecting the font, style and size for the text.
4 Selecting the position and/or direction for the title.
5 Selecting a type effect.
6 Defining the conduct of the title.

Here's what each entails.

1 Selecting an animation type: When the Text Animator button is pressed a selection of titling effect is displayed in the

Library window. Roll your mouse over the thumbnail for each type and you will see the corresponding effect demonstrated. Click on the video clip that you wish the title applied to.

2 Entering the title type: Enter the text required for the title (or credits) in the small window to the bottom left of the console desktop. Format the text as you enter it.

3 Selecting the font, style and size for the text: Click on the Font button below the text entry panel. A conventional Windows Font dialogue box will appear. Select the required font, a font style (Regular, Italic or Bold) and a size. If your text requires you can also set Right Left or Centre justification. You'll see a sample of your chosen style appear in the Sample box (note that the appearance of the text in the text entry box will not change).

4 Select the position and/or direction for the title: Use the box adjacent to the text entry box to enter the position of the title and a direction (for moving titles) by clicking in the square that you want the titles to enter from. Once you have clicked a position for the title it can be previewed in the monitor window.

5 Selecting a type effect: You can alter the look of your title text in two ways. The easiest is to click on the tab marked Effects at the base of the Library window. This displays a range of type effects featuring different colour text, some stroked (i.e. given a contrasting colour outline) and some with shadows. Double-click on a type style to apply it to your text. If you want an effect not shown use the Central Dialogue box to set the colours and the shadow. Use the sliders and buttons to alter the transparency and thickness of each.

6 Defining the conduct of the title: The conduct of the title describes how it behaves, how it enters the scene, how long it remains, and where it leaves. Each of these parameters is set by clicking on the corresponding tab at the bottom of the console and pressing one of the four buttons below the monitor window. These represent, in order, Set Effect Start Position, Set Beginning of Effect Hold Position, Set End of Effect Hold Position, Set Effect End Position. You can move the playhead to the positions required for each (note that the term 'Effect' here is synonymous with title).

Of course, if you are experienced in using image editing or illustration applications (such as Adobe Photoshop or Illustrator) you can use these to create titles. These will give you much more creative freedom in terms of the style and form of the titles enabling, for example, the use of Layer Styles (drop shadow effects and glows) and Text Warps. The drawback is that your resultant titles will be fixed – you won't have the same ability to scroll credits in the way that you can with the in-built titling features.

What to put in the titles

Remember those black-and-white movies of the 1940s where absolutely all the titles and credits were shown at the start of the movie? As well as the introductory titles a full list of the actors (then called the 'Players') would be screened, along with details of the production team and those responsible for the music. The end titles, by contrast, comprised only a caption saying 'The End'.

Today the situation is almost completely reversed. While opening titles and captions tend to be a model of brevity, end credits have become so extensive that they inevitably (and necessarily) get speeded up on their television showing to avoid hogging substantial air time.

Part of the reason for this has been the need (often now enshrined in law) to display the names of everyone involved – even peripherally – in the production of a movie. More cynically, there is an inference that the more significant or important a movie the more people will be involved and hence the longer the titles need to be.

We needn't worry about any of the politics of movie making and our titles should reflect the needs of the movie. Again it is a good idea to take inspiration from your peers. Take a look at the type of titles used in productions that are similar to yours (even if yours will ultimately be a little more modest). Examine how titles vary from genre to genre. The titles used (and the type of title) for a movie story will be quite different from those of a documentary.

Most theatrical movie titles will include:
• the principal stars
• other starring roles
• the production company
• producer
• director
• introductory scene-setting text.

Even this may be too much for your production where a more modest title will suffice:
• the name of the film
• the producer ('A Film by John Smith').

It is best to bear in mind your prospective audience. They will be wanting to see the movie or documentary. Give them the important and relevant information and no more.

Of course, you will be proud of your production and will want to promote yourself and those involved in it. It is best to leave these credits until the end and keep them brief also. When your movie is being played on a video, CD-ROM or DVD you don't want your audience to switch off immediately!

Special effects

When digital image editing software – the likes of which are represented today by applications such as Photoshop or PhotoSuite – first appeared it enabled photographers to enhance photographs on their desktop computer and produce photographic quality prints in a matter of minutes. It also gave rise to the easy application of special effects (known as filters) and suddenly quite acceptable images could be transformed into psychedelic nightmares. Showing no other creative skill than the user being able to press a filter's 'Apply' button, these images filled photographic magazines for a short while before their uncreative origins were sussed. In fact these innocuous little effects helped give digital photography – in its early days – something of a bad name.

As time passed photographers learnt the true power of effect filters and used them in the creation of better and more powerful imagery. In this more mature creative environment they are used more sparingly and always to improve an image.

What has this to do with digital video editing? Well, many of the filters available to photographers have video equivalents and most software applications include a selection of them. Like their photographic equivalents, these special effects include the useful, the shocking and the downright bizarre. And like that apocryphal child in the sweet shop we are bound, on discovery, to try to use them all in the belief that we are the first to do so!

Of course it is wrong to condemn special effects merely because of the way they are used and abused. In fact, there are many that can be used to enhance our work. Both iMovie and VideoWave include core sets that deserve closer scrutiny.

In iMovie you can see the range of effects by selecting the Effects tab at the base of the Shelf window.

VideoWave's comprehensive set of effects is found spread through the Darkroom, Special Effects, Video Mixer and TimeWarp rooms. You can select each of these from the Mode Selector

Darkroom effects

Both iMovie and VideoWave feature effects that, broadly speaking, duplicate the effects normally produced when traditional darkroom processes are applied to film. Here's a selection of those on offer:

- Black and white: (perhaps rather obviously) turns colour footage into black and white.

- Sepia tone: converts footage to black and white then applies an amber sepia tone, to give a 'nostalgic' feel to the images. No film footage – so far as I am aware – ever turned true sepia (although old black-and-white prints did) but the effect is used to impart an 'aged' look to movies that most viewers seem happy to accept.

- Adjust colours: This is a quick way to pep up the colours in a scene (if those colours are a little flat) or to knock back colours that would otherwise appear too garish. By using slider controls you can increase the colour saturation in a scene or, conversely, reduce the amount of colour. You can also alter the colour balance (to compensate for an incorrect White Balance setting, for example).

- Brightness/contrast. Another obvious effect. This too uses slider controls to alter the brightness of a scene or to vary the contrast. The contrast control can be useful for nudging up the contrast in scenes that are lit by, for example, overcast skies. In practice the two controls are used in tandem with, say, the brightness reduced slightly and the contrast increased to give a 'flatter' scene that is more easily reproduced on screen.

- Sharpen. By increasing the perceived (rather than actual) sharpness video that is slightly soft or out of focus can be made to look better focused. You should use this filter only once. Though you will be able to use it repeatedly it will quickly generate damaging image artefacts that will degrade your image.

- Soft focus. Unlike blurring (which is, in effect, the opposite of sharpening) soft focus introduces a soft dream-like haze while maintaining overall sharpness. It's an ideal effect to use if you are aiming to give shots a romantic feel.

A range of special effects is shown on colour plates 4 and 5.

Applying special effects

Special effects can be applied to a complete clip, an entire video or more selectively. Applying to a clip or video is achieved by dragging and dropping the appropriate effect to the selected clip. This typically applies the effect from start to finish of that clip. You can, however, fade an effect in and out during a scene. In iMovie use the Effect In and Effect Out sliders to set a time before and after the effect is applied to the clip. In VideoWave you can use the same controls as we used to add and manipulate titles (titles, as you may recall, are treated in VideoWave as a type of special effect).

Do note that unlike photographic filters (that can be applied to selected areas of an image) the video equivalent is applied to the whole frame area.

iMovie special effects

A limited range of further effects is offered in iMovie and on the Apple Website (see p.235).

VideoWave special effects

VideoWave boasts a more comprehensive range of special effects than iMovie with three further rooms of special effects. The Special Effect room contains more wacky effects, samples of which are shown on the next page.

The Time Warp and Video Mixer rooms can be used to create quite different special effects. Time Warp speeds up or slows down a video clip to give fast play or slow motion effects respectively.

To use Time Warp:

1 Choose the video clip that you wish to alter the replay of and press the Time Warp icon on the Mode Selector.
2 Set the TimeWarp Factor between fast and slow.
3 Alter the Motion Blending control to help smooth the motion in the lengthened or shortened video. This prevents the jerkiness that often results when video play times are altered.
4 Select a filename for the revised clip (a systematic name is created by default by appending '–warped' to the original name.
5 Click Start to begin rendering the new clip.

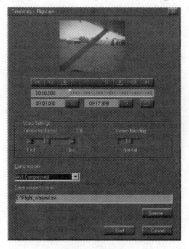

This is also a good way of lengthening scenes that do not have any significant moving subjects.

Video Mixer combines two video clips in a single scene. This can be a simple picture in picture mix or a more complex chroma keying (sometimes called blue screen) where a colour is selected in one image and used to superimpose elements of the second scene. It's the same technique as used extensively in television to superimpose, for example, a weather forecaster over a weather map.

more visual effects

The fact that we are working in a digital domain means we have greater flexibility on combining movie footage with other digital media. And, conversely, we can also extract material from our video to use in other ways.

Using still images

Though it sounds slightly ironic, still images can be very effective elements of a movie production. Still images have many uses: they can, for example, be used as titles or as backgrounds for titles. Transitions and scene linking is another use. A collection of historic still images of a locale, carefully mixed, could be used to introduce a video about that same locale today. At a more pedestrian level we can even produce slideshows of still images using video editing software, adding soundtracks and special effects to enhance the show.

So how do we acquire still images in a form suitable for inclusion in our digital video production?

Digital stills cameras

The most obvious source is a digital stills camera. Though once a poor relation of conventional film-based cameras, digital cameras can now boast quality to rival these in most areas. With regard to incorporating images in digital video movies the digital still camera has the clear advantage of delivering images that can be used pretty well immediately, without any format conversions. If you do not already own a digital stills camera, there is no longer any excuse not to. Apart from providing valuable additional imagery for your movie projects, they are a great replacement for your old stills camera.

There is now an extensive range in both quality and price, from simple point and shoot models through to professional systems capable of the highest quality images. Though other factors are also important, it is the resolution of the camera that determines the detail in the image and the quality of the results.

Basic cameras offer somewhat limited resolution (typically 640 × 480 pixels) which is a little less than that of the DV format. Many of these cameras also function as webcams, delivering low-resolution video over Internet connections. These are likely not to offer either the quality of performance to enhance your video work.

Cameras with resolution of over 2 million pixels (called 2 megapixel) are probably the minimum requirement and, due to the onward march of top-end models, inexpensive. Features such as a zoom lens and macro setting (for extreme close-ups) make the more sophisticated models in this class very useful for gathering images across a range of situations.

even comparatively basic digital cameras are ideal for video projects

If you are willing to spend a little more 5-megapixel models can offer image and print quality very similar to that offered by 35mm models. Still images of A4 or even A3 size will be possible and while this resolution is likely to be overkill with regard to video use, the flexibility of the cameras (and the high level of specification typical of these cameras) make them very valuable tools. The higher price can often be justified as these cameras can often replace conventional 35mm models for general stills photography.

high resolution cameras can also replace conventional 35mm cameras

All but the most basic cameras save images to a memory card (SmartMedia, CompactFlash, Memory Stick, XD-Picture Card or SD card, depending on the camera model). Dubbed 'digital film' (although as they are re-recordable, this term is not entirely accurate) these can store a large number of images, the exact number determined by the capacity of the card and the degree of image compression used.

memory cards

Downloading images to the computer is simple and can be achieved either by attaching the camera directly (typically using a USB lead) or by inserting the memory card into a card reader attached to the computer. Bespoke download software is provided by the camera manufacturers and many image editing applications feature download facilities. For example, Apple's iPhoto, the still photo equivalent to iMovie, is particularly effective, making the process of download, cataloguing, editing (admittedly on a modest scale) and print creation very simple indeed.

card reader

Scanners

If you have a large collection of prints, negatives, transparencies or other flat artwork a scanner is the ideal solution to getting these into your computer. Most scanners are flatbed models, comprising a glass plate (around A4 size typically, A3 in some models) upon which the artwork is placed. This is then scanned (in a similar manner to a photocopier) to a digital file.

Though some models offer a very high resolution that is sufficient to provide an appropriately high resolution scan of negatives and transparencies, dedicated slide scanners are often a better bet if you have a large collection of slides – or negatives – to scan. These are better configured to the characteristics of these media.

a flatbed scanner (left) and a slide scanner

PhotoCD and PictureCD

If you have a smaller collection of images or prefer to use a conventional camera for your photographic images, the CD-based formats PhotoCD and PictureCD provide an economic and convenient source of digitized images. PhotoCD is designed more for the enthusiast or professional photographer and offers digitized images at a series of alternate resolutions. The CD can be produced when a film is processed or retrospectively from a selection of images (which can be mixed slide and negative and from 35mm or larger film).

PictureCD offers a more modest 6-megapixel file size from 35mm film and proportionately less from APS film. It is not available to larger film sizes. PictureCDs are normally produced when a film is processed along with, or instead of, conventional prints. It is an automatic process, so is available from many one-hour photoprocessors.

a PhotoCD (left) and a PictureCD

Video camera

Don't overlook the still image feature of your digital video camera. Where this is generated as a still image recorded onto the tape (usually for around five seconds) this will be downloaded as a video clip – just like true video clips. The true still image mode offered by some cameras saves the image to a memory card in much the same way as with a digital stills camera. It can also be downloaded to your computer in the same way, via the camera or an external card reader. Though resolution of these still images is modest in still image terms it will still be quite sufficient for video uses.

Image editing software

There's no reason why a still image should not be imported directly into your video editing application but you may want to manipulate the image first. Such manipulations may be modest – for example changing the size – or more complex, involving changing the content of the image. The software for this, like video editing applications, varies in price and features. Often you'll find appropriate software included in the software package that comes with digital stills cameras and scanners. There is not the space to discuss the opportunities of digital photography here – it would take a whole book. Indeed it has. *Teach Yourself Digital Photography* provides an excellent introduction to the process of image editing.

If you don't currently own an image editing application here's a run-down of the top applications.

- Adobe Photoshop: The top application that has become virtual industry standard. It includes every conceivable feature required for image editing, pre-press and printing work and Web graphics. For the dedicated image editing enthusiast it is unrivalled, though for creating images for your video it could be considered overkill. It also commands a very high price. It is available for Mac and Windows users.

- Jasc Paint Shop Pro: A very well specified Windows-only application that is ideal for creating powerful images. It is more economically priced and this price includes companion product Animation Shop, dedicated to the creation of Web animations.

- Corel Photo-Paint: Another major and comprehensive image editing application that is available as a stand-alone application and also as part of Corel's CorelDRAW! for Windows and Corel Graphics Suite (Mac).

- Ulead PhotoImpact: A powerful image editor that is particularly adept at combining images with special effects, with drag and drop funtionality applied extensively. Very useful for achieving 'quick' fixes.

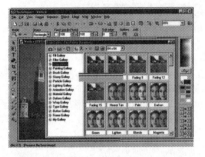

- Roxio PhotoSuite: From the same stable as VideoWave, PhotoSuite takes a project-based approach to the construction of images and graphics. The stepwise approach is particularly appropriate for those who are inexperienced at image editing.

Some simple image edits

Though image editing itself is also outside the scope of this book, here are some simple corrections that will yield better images for your video productions. These are not specific to any one image editing application and can be found in all the applications listed above.

- Automatic corrections: Sometimes called Quick Fix tools these are not applied automatically to all your images but rather make automatic adjustments to certain image parameters. For example, there are commands such as 'Auto Contrast' that, somewhat obviously, alters the contrast in an image to prevent areas of too high a contrast. There are equivalent commands that adjust the colour balance and even brightness. These usually work very well and are an expedient way of fixing images. They are less successful at correcting images that have been shot with deliberately abnormal colour or contrast distributions that you wish to preserve. They can, in cases such as brightly coloured sunsets, reduce the impact.

- Brightness/contrast: This is a control that is similar to the video correction effect detailed on p.95. You can use simple sliders to increase or decrease the brightness and/or contrast. Unlike in the video implementation of this control you can select a specific part of an image (using selection tools) and apply the corrections only to that area.

- Colour and colour balance: You'll find several controls that can be used to alter the colour saturation (again reducing or increasing) and even change the hues of an image or selection.

Colour Balance controls enable colour casts (such as those introduced when taking photographs in certain lighting conditions) to be neutralized or, should you need to, enhanced.

- Sharpen and blur: Sharpen controls introduce perceived sharpness to your image and can give the impression of a slightly sharper image. They can be used successfully with images that are not critically sharp. It is important to note that a sharpened image will not reveal the fine detail of the original scene that was not recorded due to imprecise focusing. Blur controls enable you to increase the amount of blur but are more often used to introduce motion blurs (to convey the impression of motion).

Importing images into a video editing application

Because they too are digital, video editing applications make little distinction between a still and moving image and can handle each in much the same way. The main difference is that still images will need to be imported image by image, rather than en-mass as with digital video.

Importing images using iMovie

iMovie will accept still images that have been stored in one of several image file formats including JPEG, BMP, GIF, PICT and Photoshop.

1 Select File menu ➜ Import File.
2 Identify the file and click Import. The file will appear on iMovie's shelf.

3 By default the still image will last five seconds. To alter the duration select Edit menu → Preferences → Import and enter a new duration (the nominal range is 0.5 sec to 60 sec).

Note that if the image size or format does not match that of the iMovie frame you will see a black border or black stripes. If it is important that the image fills the window (and it usually is) you will need to use an image editing application to resize the image accordingly.

Once the image is on the shelf you can regard it as you would any video clip. Drag it to the timeline and append it to (or insert between) existing video clips. You can then apply transitions to the entry and exit points and place titles or effects over it.

Importing images using VideoWave

VideoWave accepts images in the formats JPEG, BMP, PostScript (EPS), PhotoCD (PCD), FlashPix (FPX), TIFF and Photoshop.

1 Select File menu → Import File.
2 Identify the file and click Import. The imported image will appear in the Library.

Images are identified in the Library by a small painter's palette icon in the corner of the image thumbnail.

Extracting a still image from video footage

Just as we can incorporate a still image in our video so we can extract a still image from our movie. The result will be a still image (of approximately 1.25 megabytes, 768 × 576 pixels) that can be printed or edited (in an image editing application)

Extracting a still image using iMovie

A still image can be extracted from any point in a video clip or movie.

1 Select the clip or movie from which you wish to extract the still image.
2 Move the playhead to the appropriate point in the movie. By selecting the corresponding clip from the timeline you will be

able to get better accuracy if it is important to extract a specific frame.

3 Select File menu → Save Frame As and specify a location for the saved frame. You can save your image as a PICT or JPEG format file.

You can also save the image as a still clip, which will be placed on the shelf in the same manner as an imported image. Select Edit menu → Create Still Clip when the playhead is at the appropriate position.

Extracting a still image from VideoWave

Still images can be extracted from a movie in VideoWave in the Cutting Room.

1 Select the clip that you wish to extract a still image from and select the Cutting Room icon from the Mode Selector.

2 Move the playhead to the position of the frame that you wish to extract as an image (you can use the Previous Frame and Next Frame buttons if you wish to select a precise frame).

3 Select the Extract box on the Console and click Image to open the Extract Images dialogue box.

4 Click Extract to create a still image and save the image to the Library. Click Export to export the image to any other folder.

Importing movies from your digital stills camera

Many digital stills cameras feature a movie mode that records short clips of video (at somewhat lower resolution than for still images) with or without sound. Files are stored on the camera's memory card in AVI format. You can import these into your video editing application in the same way as a still image.

- Importing AVI files into iMovie: As these video clips are normally stored in AVI format (a format that cannot be directly imported into iMovie) you will need to convert them first to DV format. This will require a subsidiary application such as QuickTime Pro (standard QuickTime does not include transcoding features). See Chapter 8 for more details of QuickTime Pro and formats conversion.
- Importing into VideoWave: AVI files can be imported directly into VideoWave. To import an AVI file from your camera it is best to first copy the file to your computer's hard disc (this is not an essential step, but it prevents any communications conflicts that might occur when downloading direct from the camera). Then select File ➜ Insert Video. Identify the AVI file you wish to import and then click Import. A thumbnail, representing your AVI movie, will appear in the Library. Do note that the quality from these AVI files can be far inferior to that of DV footage and their disparate origins will be very obvious when clips of each type are combined.

The best results from a digital stills camera movie mode will be from cameras sporting the so-called Third Generation Super CCD (3G SuperCCD) from Fujifilm. By special processing techniques and pixel combinations these cameras can offer VGA quality images (compared with the quarter VGA of other models) and frame rates of up to 30 frames per second.

adding sound

In this chapter you will learn
- about using music in a production
- how to add a narrative
- about sound effects.

There have never been any true 'silent' movies. Those vintage films without a soundtrack always had an organist (or some other instrumentalist) to provide a live themed accompaniment. Even those silent Super-8 holiday movies had an impromptu (and sometimes argumentative) narration provided by the featured holidaymakers. Hence we expect a movie to be an experience for both our eyes and ears. The only difference is that we now have tools to make the audio component of our movie as impressive as the visuals.

The sound of our movies can comprise a number of elements. There will be the ambient sounds – those recorded along with the video and sometimes called native sound (later, when we examine video recording technique we'll look more closely at the options for ambient recordings). Added sounds are likely to consist of music, narration (or voice over) and sound effects.

Using music

Like so much else about video editing and post-production there is nothing difficult about adding music – finding appropriate music is perhaps the more tricky aspect. It is the music, perhaps more than the visuals that can add mood to movies. Before your audience sees a single shot of video the music can have already set the tone and the expectation.

The legal stuff

Before going any further we need to take a look at the subject of copyright. Though we can use many euphemistic terms to describe adding music to the soundtrack of a movie, if that music is from a third party artist we come up against the question of copyright.

Virtually all music, other than original works created by you, is covered implicitly by copyright legislation. This exists not to stifle your creativity but to protect the rights of those who have created the music in the first place. To use copyright material in your production you will need authority from the copyright holder and, almost inevitably, you will have to pay a fee.

In practice gaining such authority and making an agreement would be unfeasible. It would (through the legal necessities) prove too expensive for most home productions. Instead consider using music designed specifically for the purpose.

There are countless albums of royalty-free music produced as background music. Rather than being copyright-free, the copyright owner licences you to use the music in any appropriate manner that usually includes distributing movies for outright profit. These musicians are no philanthropists; rather they gain payments through the sale of CDs of their music or for paid downloads from the Internet.

It should be noted that by the strict interpretation of the copyright laws any use of copyright material is protected. It is often said that if a production is for your own or your family's consumption then you can use any material with impunity. This is not the case; whether the production is to be screened on TV or viewed in more intimate surroundings the law is still the law.

In practice it is very unlikely that any organization will pursue you for using your favourite CD track on your modest domestic production but you still need to be aware of the implications. And if you have greater aspirations for your work, it makes sense to consider alternatives.

Creating your own music

One such alternative if you have even modest musical abilities is to create your own music – it is not necessary to write a concerto as (for background music in particular) the emphasis needs to be more on a clear melody.

If you do not have such abilities there is another option for creating unique music. Computer-generated music has come a long way from the surreal cacophonies once used to show the capabilities of contemporary computers (which, from the sound output were not particularly strong with regard to music ...). Applications such as Sonic Foundry's Acid Music help you create impressive music in a range of styles. And if you've no experience of writing music whatsoever, don't worry! Acid takes care of all of that.

Using royalty-free and stock music

As we have just mentioned music collections designed for use on video productions are widely available. These are often found in themed collections (such as 'Chases', 'Mediterranean Music' or 'Suspense') and include a wide range of alternatives within each category. They will also be of differing durations. You many find material that lasts only 15 seconds through to long concertos. You can even get 'endless' tracks that are easily mixed so that they appear to play continually.

There is some variation in licensing arrangements for discs and it is advisable to check before buying that these are compatible with your requirements. The normal arrangement is for unlimited use with regard to video production. This means you can use the material freely whether your production is intended for limited distribution or more widespread. But you couldn't, unless otherwise advised, use it as background music at a party. Take note of any caveats – some restrict you geographically (you can use the material freely on productions distributed in Europe but not on any distributed in North America, for example).

The drawbacks to royalty-free and stock music are that it is not unique – it has (and will) be used by many others in a variety of different situations – and that it has not been specifically designed for the duration and the tempo of your production.

Check the classified ads in the video and camcorder magazines for sources of music.

Editing music

Whether you need to edit your music (or other elements of the movie's soundtrack) will depend upon the level of sophistication required. A significant amount of editing can be achieved with the most modest of video editing applications but if you need something more there are plenty of audio editing applications available.

Audio editing is very similar in both principle and practice to video editing. Audio tracks can be trimmed and cropped to the correct length or the cut away material. Likewise Cut, Copy and Paste commands perform in the same way as the video equivalents.

Though video editors include video mixing features, audio editing applications make more extensive use of their mixers to enable both the mixing of consecutive sound clips and the creation of more elaborate sounds.

Using a narrative

Documentary movie productions will generally feature some sort of narrative, ranging from short explanatory clips through to a more extensive accompaniment. Should you cut your movie to accompany the narrative, or write the narrative to fit with your video cut?

There is, of course, no easy answer to this. As a general rule it would be fair to say that visually led subject matter should be editing to suit those visuals. Where there is a clear story to be told and the visual matter supports this story then the story should take preference, dictating the assembly of the video clips.

Sound effects

The term sound effect is generally used to describe sounds added to the soundtrack to increase the perceived sense of realism and build atmosphere. Thunderclaps, smashing glass and footsteps are typical. It also describes those effects that are more dubious and controversial in their application such as applause, laughter and even drum rolls. Video editing applications tend to feature a limited range of the most used (and most useable) sound effects which are actually quite useful in pepping up a video. More impressive effects can be found on specialist effects CDs and on the Web. If you have appropriate facilities – such as a stereo tape or minidisc recorder – you can create your own bespoke effects.

Adding sound to your movie

Adding sound to an iMovie production

iMovie provides a selection of sound handling tools that enable you to import sound from a range of sources and then edit and adjust these sounds as required for your movie. The audio element of iMovie comprises the two soundtracks indicated on the timeline (when the lower tab is pressed) and the Audio palette containing a library of sound effects and recording tools. You can display this by pressing the Audio button below the Shelf.

Exploring the Audio palette
The Audio palette comprise three panes. These enable you to (from the top) add a sound effect, add a voice recording and add pre-recorded music.

1 Sound Effects: iMovie includes a small collection of sound effects comprising those effects – such as applause, clapping and drum rolls – that could be used in almost any domestic video. Despite being somewhat clichéd they are nonetheless useful embellishments for a modest production. A more extensive range of effects is available (for free) at the iMovie website (www.apple.com/imovie/freestuff). To use a sound effect first select it from the list. Double click and the clip will be played. Next drag it to one of the soundtracks on the timeline. The duration of each effect is given in the menu.

2 Voice Recordings: The Voice Recording pane makes it simple to record a narrative track. You can start the recording at any point on the movie by moving the playhead to the appropriate point on the timeline and then pressing the Record Voice button. Obviously it requires that a microphone is attached to the computer or that any built-in microphone is enabled.

3 Recorded Music: This option makes it possible to add music from a commercial CD. See below for full details on how to import music using this feature.

AIFF Files

When you import sound files iMovie expects them to be in Audio Interchange File Format (AIFF – sometimes called AIF). Music and sound effects recorded in this format are widely available on the Web and there are also CDs of AIF music (both commercial and royalty-free) available from specialist suppliers. However, there is a wide range (that is changed or added to periodically) on the iMovie website. You'll find sound effects (such as wind and rain) through to looping music in categories such as Back Beat, Offbeat, Ominous and Techno.

AIFF files are imported by selecting Import File from the iMovie File menu and choosing the relevant file. Once you click Import the file will appear on the soundtrack on the timeline.

If your original material is not in AIFF format don't worry. The following sections will show you how to import sound files from the most common sources, CD and MP3.

Importing sound from CD

CDs probably comprise the most common source of music or other sound that you are likely to use. Importing CD tracks is easy.

1 With iMovie open, select the Audio palette.
2 Insert the appropriate CD into your computer's CD or DVD drive.
3 After a few seconds the CD will appear in the palette with the tracks (along with their duration) listed. Normally these will appear as 'Track 1, Track 2 etc., but they may appear by name if you have the appropriate naming software installed on your computer.
4 Use the play controls to cue the music you wish to use (you can play the track and listen in using the computer's speakers).

Audio CD 1	37:33:00
Track 1	02:38:00
Track 2	03:47:00
Track 3	03:38:00
Track 4	02:24:00
Track 5	02:48:00
Track 6	04:07:00
Track 7	02:31:00
Track 8	01:37:00
Track 9	03:12:00
Track 10	03:54:00
Track 11	03:10:00

Record Music

5 Click Record Music at the start point and press the same button (then relabelled 'Stop') when you want to end the recording.

6 As the track plays you will see it being added to the lower of the two audio tracks in the timeline.

Importing MP3 files

Though AIF/AIFF files are the standard file format for audio recognized by iMovie, chances are much of your music will be stored as MP3 files. MP3 represents an ideal way to store music (and, for that matter, speech) as it provides high quality output yet file sizes that can be 10 per cent those of the equivalent CD track. There are also a great number of royalty-free tracks on the Internet that can be downloaded easily in MP3 format. The easiest way to convert an MP3 file to AIFF is to use QuickTime Player Pro.

1 Open the QuickTime Player.
2 If a player is not visible select File → New Player. A new player window will appear.
3 Select File → Open Movie and select the MP3 file that you wish to convert.
4 At this stage you may want to review the piece of music and perhaps edit it to the appropriate length (saving time and disc space).
5 Choose File → Export and in the pop-up menu select Sound.
6 Save the file. Back in iMovie use File → Import File to import it into iMovie. The file will appear on the soundtrack on the timeline.

Note that if you wish to import an entire track you can drag the track from the CD window to the timeline soundtrack. The message 'Importing Audio CD track ...' will appear as the track is imported and laid to the appropriate soundtrack. You can add a track to either of the sound tracks.

Editing music on the soundtracks

Once music has been imported to the soundtracks you can edit and manipulate it. Begin by clicking on the appropriate track to select it. You can now give the track a meaningful name (if it doesn't already have one) by typing it in the Audio Selection box above the timeline. You can now fade the music in and/or out by using the buttons at the base of the timeline. The volume control between the buttons sets the Relative Volume. This can be used to alter the volume of the selected music so that it does not dominate other sounds, such as the original soundtrack or any narration.

You can place the music track by selecting it and then dragging it to the required position. To position the track precisely move the playhead (indicated by the vertical line through the timeline) to the start and then use the arrow keys to move the playhead and the track to the required position. The start point will be shown in the Monitor window.

Note that each music track features a triangular marker at the start and finish. If you move these along the track only the portion of the track between them will play.

If you wish you can also lock a soundtrack to a particular part of a movie clip. This is essential if you are going to make changes to the movie clips; adding, removing or editing clips will result in the clips and sound moving out of synchronization and your hard-won cueing will be lost. Here's how to lock the audio in position:

1 Move the playhead to the start of the audio clip and check that the appropriate frame of video is displayed.
2 Select Advanced menu ➔ Lock Audio Clip at Playhead.

Now no matter what alterations are made to elements on the timeline the sound and vision are locked together. If you need to remove a lock you can do so by selecting Unlock Audio Clip from the Advanced menu.

You can also split a video clip containing a soundtrack recorded 'live' into separate video and audio tracks. You might use this when adding cutaways wherein the soundtrack continues uninterrupted throughout a movie but different video scenes are added. Split a clip into audio and video by selecting Advanced ➔ Extract Audio. The video clip will remain on the timeline and the audio will be added to the lower audio track. At this stage if you were to replay the movie you would not notice a difference. However, were you to substitute the original video clip with another and replay you would see the alternate scene but with the original soundtrack throughout.

Adding sound to a VideoWave production

VideoWave supports sound files in a range of formats: WAV, MP2, MP3 and CD Audio. Any sound file in one of these formats can be imported directly into VideoWave where they are stored in the Audio Library. You can view the contents of the Audio Library by clicking on the Audio tab at the base of the Library panel. Sound functions are handled by the VideoWave

Shot types

extra-long shot

long shot

medium shot

medium close-up

close-up

extra close-up

Interfaces

VideoWave

iMovie

VideoImpression

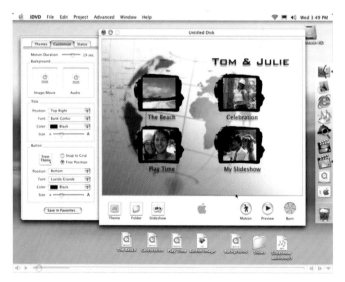

iDVD

Video editing special effects (Basic Set)

original image

black and white

sepia

soft focus

adjust colours

ripple filter

Lighting types

tungsten lighting (white balance set for daylight)

tungsten lighting (white balance set for tungsten)

ambient light: suitably corrected, ambient room lighting adds more character to the shot

mixed lighting: the mixed lighting of this theatrical shot is no problem for a camera with white balance set to 'auto'

Windows Media Player can be configured with different 'skins'
while these rarely enhance the production they do have a certain novelty value
some, however, do have a smaller than desirable picture area

component called the Audio Studio. VideoWave permits a maximum of six audio tracks that can be used to add, for example, additional ambient noises, narration, background music and special effects.

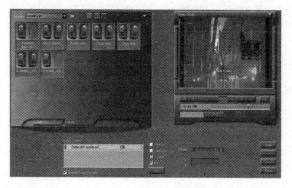

Adding a sound file to the Library

To add a file to the Library ensure first that the source of the sound file (whether a local hard disc, network disc or CD) is available to the computer.

1 Click on the Audio tab, as described above, to display the Audio Library. This will already contain some audio tracks that are provided with the VideoWave program.
2 Select the Arrowhead (to the top right of the Audio Library) and select Add Files from the menu.
3 Use the browser to identify the file required and click on Open. The file will be imported and a thumbnail appended to those in the Library.

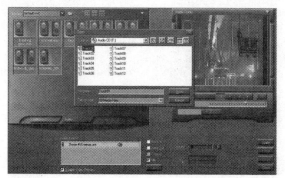

Adding a voice over or commentary

VideoWave does not feature an in-built option for recording and adding a narrative track directly. To add a voice over (or subsidiary ambient sounds) you will first need to record the required material using an alternate application. Windows Sound Recorder is an adequate, if basic, application that is freely available. You can store your sound file (in WAV format) directly to the computer's hard disc ready to import into VideoWave.

Adding an audio track to a video clip

You can use the Audio Studio to add one or more audio tracks to any video clip. If the clip is shorter than the audio track, the track will continue playing over following clips. Here's how to link an audio track with a video clip:

1 Select the video clip to which you wish to add an audio track from the storyboard. The first frame of that video clip will appear in the monitor window.

2 Select the Audio Studio icon to display the available audio clips and the Audio Tracks control panel on the desktop.

3 Drag the required audio track from the Library to the control panel. Its title will appear in the Audio Tracks window.

4 You can now choose how you want this track played. Select from the Audio Playback buttons whether you want a fade in, fade out or both. Pressing the Loop button turns your audio track into an endless track, repeating indefinitely. Mix will mix this audio with others associated with the video clip. Deselecting the Mix button will mute the sound.

5 Alter the volume of the audio track using the slider. This will set the volume relative to the original sound. For background music you may choose to set this to a low or moderate level; for more forthright sound a higher level may be appropriate.

6 Adjust the position of the playhead (below the monitor window) to the point at which you want the audio to begin. Select the Set Effect Start Position button to set the audio to start at this position.

7 Click the Apply button to link the sound and video at the selected point.

Now review the video and the associated audio track. Note that if you need to alter the start position you can do so easily. Select the video track again and, using the Audio Studio, set the playhead to the new position and repeat steps 6 and 7 above.

Splitting sound and video

Like iMovie, VideoWave allows the audio component of a video clip to be separated from the video for cutaway use, for example. To do this in VideoWave you'll need to work in the Cutting Room. Select the video clip that you wish to separate and then the Cutting Room icon. Select Audio from the Extract controls at the bottom of the screen. Give the audio file that is created a name and specify a location to save it.

09 publishing our movie

In this chapter you will learn:
- how to create a master tape
- about exporting video to different media
- how to publish your video.

Now our movie production is complete in terms of the sound and the visuals we need to consider how to publish it. 'Publishing' sounds a somewhat grandiose term for our modest production but whether we intend to share the movie with a few friends or make it available to a larger audience the options – and many of the problems – are the same.

The principal distribution options are:

- Exporting to videotape. This includes copying back to digital videotape to create a master videotape and to more widely available consumer formats such as the ubiquitous VHS.
- Exporting to disc-based media. This describes not only CD-ROM (that is conventionally replayed on a computer) but also DVD and VideoCD, discs that enable our productions to be enjoyed on a conventional TV.
- The Web. Emailing, website posting and streaming are further options for distributing our movies.

In this chapter we look at the opportunities offered by exporting to videotape and disc-based media. In the next we will look at Web-based distribution and also the technologies employed. It is important to note that each medium has both strengths and weaknesses and that it is likely that a movie presentation will be recorded on more than one if it is to receive the widest exposure.

Creating a master tape

Before we set about distributing our movie it is important that we create a master videotape that will be the source for all our copies. This needs to be made on a format that is both robust and does not compromise quality. Once we have produced this master videotape we can delete the copy on our computer to free up the hard disc ready for the next production.

The most practical 'robust format' is actually the same digital videotape that we used to record footage in the first place. To create your master tape there is no better way than to copy it back onto the same tape (whether DV, Digital8 or MicroMV) using the same digital camera. This is why we emphasized, early on, the importance of selecting a camera that includes a bi-directional FireWire connector.

A master tape from iMovie

Exporting the finished video from iMovie is simple.

1 Select File ➔ Export Movie to open the Export dialogue box.
2 Open the pull down menu and select Camera as the Export device. Note the small information panel that advises the duration of the video to be exported and also reminds you to check your camera has a tape loaded.

3 Select a Wait period. This is the time that iMovie will wait before it starts exporting the movie to enable the camera to start up and configure itself to receive data. The default setting is five seconds (which is appropriate for most cameras) but you may need to increase this to ensure that the start of the recording is not truncated.
4 Also type in the number of seconds of black to be added to the start and end of the movie. This will add a specified number of seconds of black screen prior to and after the movie export. You do not need to add black but it does make for a smoother video presentation, avoiding an abrupt start or finish.
5 Click on Export. Exporting takes place in real time (a 20-minute movie will take 20 minutes to copy).

A master tape from VideoWave

In VideoWave the process is similarly simple:

1 Select the Output to Video button on the Mode Selector bar.

2 The Settings Panel will appear on the desktop.

3 Click on Begin to start the download (you may have to start your camera manually depending on the model).

4 You can pause the recording at the first frame by clicking on the respective button. This pauses the playback until the camera (or recorder) is ready. You can also pause the video on the last frame.

It is a good idea when copying material to or from a video camera to use the mains adaptor to power the camera. If you use battery power there is always a risk that the battery power will be insufficient and the recording truncated.

If you plan to make a great deal of use of your movie-making skills it could be more effective to make your master recordings using a specialized digital video deck. Looking for all the world like a conventional home video deck (and with many of the same features, including the ability to make timer recordings) these machines can help reduce the wear and tear on your camcorder and – in the case of DV models – can use full-sized DV tapes which offer extended recording times. Though not cheap they can ultimately prove economic. Digital VHS (D-VHS) recorders (discussed below) provide another recording alternative although the data recorded (with regard to scenes and time/date) may not be so comprehensive.

Once you have created your master recording it is a good idea to make at least one further copy. Think of these master copies as back-up copies which have the same purpose as the back-ups we take (or often don't take) of valuable computer data. Should something disastrous happen to our master, then we've an identical copy from which any subsequent copies can be made.

A common question that arises at this point is 'should we retain our original recordings?' This is a difficult question to answer. On one hand you might argue that you will need to keep all originals just in case you might need them to rework an existing production. On the other, the chances of this actually happening (particularly if you have taken care to produce a technically perfect production) are small. And should this need arise you will generally find that when you transfer the recording back to the computer it will be divided back into component scenes automatically during the process.

Exporting to videotape

There is no doubt that conventional VHS videotape represents the most effective way to distribute 'original' copies of your production. Very few recipients will be unable to replay a VHS tape and the tape itself is an economic distribution medium.

If we ignore proprietary improvements and quality shifts due to different playing speeds, there are three grades of VHS video available.

Standard VHS is the most basic and is the format used by and replayable on all VCRs. It has comparatively low resolution (240 lines) but is quite acceptable for most applications. This is the format used for most time-shift recordings and also that used for commercially produced video. Most viewers are quite happy to watch a video recorded at this quality but the more exacting home cinema enthusiast is less likely to be impressed.

The intermediate quality Super VHS (SVHS) offers 400-line resolution but at the cost of such recordings not being easily replayed back on standard VHS decks (only certain non-SVHS models offer the special replay mode that replays SVHS recordings and these do so at only 240-line resolution). SVHS represents the highest quality in conventional video formats but to get the best reproduction you will need a television that offers a dedicated SVHS signal connector or a modified SCART connector that can accommodate SVHS signals. SVHS VCRs will replay SVHS and VHS tapes.

Digital VHS (D-VHS) is a further evolution of the format that allows the recording of programming and video in digital format. D-VHS VCRs feature multiple recording options for different data rates. It can also be used to record the raw bitstream of digital television broadcasts. In fact, D-VHS stands for Data-VHS rather than Digital-VHS, but the latter term tends to be that in common usage. D-VHS VCRs can replay all other VHS tapes.

Clearly the format we use when exporting, or copying, a digital video recording will depend upon the type of VCR that the recipient possesses and, in general, this will be standard VHS quality. D-VHS will offer the best quality and shares the other virtues of digital video recording, but there will be, for the moment at least, very few who can enjoy the quality offered.

How do we go about exporting video to a domestic VCR? We've two options. We can copy the original video from our computer disc or we can use our master videotape.

It is difficult to copy direct from a computer as, in general, the connectors required to link to a VCR are not provided as standard. We have a better chance if we have an A to D converter (either an external device or inbuilt). Most of these feature two-way communications that will allow our digital video to be output in analogue form.

The connections will normally comprise one for each of the two audio channels and one for the video signal. If our equipment supports SVHS the video signal will require a special 'S' connector that carries the two channels of video signal required for this format.

Most of us, however, won't have a converter and will need to rely on our camcorder as the source for our VHS copies. As well as digital inputs and outputs, camcorders incorporate analogue video-out connections. These are normally used when replaying the video through a television. To copy a video from a tape in the camcorder to a VCR you simply connect to the VCR inputs rather than the television. You can, of course, monitor the recording in progress by selecting the VCR channel on the television.

Note that copying videotapes in this manner can be a laborious process as all domestic transfer equipment works in real time (i.e. each copy of a 20-minute video will take 20 minutes to produce). It can also take its toll on the camcorder's delicate (and expensive to repair) mechanism. If you need to make a large number of copies it can prove more economic to trust the job to a duplicating house. Here your master tape (most will accept a digital master tape) can be copied simultaneously, sometimes at speed to create any number of copies. Most duplicating houses offer additional services such as printed sleeves or even case notes. Check your local classified directory, favourite Web search engine or the classified ads in movie-making magazines for information on prices.

Signal loop through

Some camcorders can act as surrogate A to D converters when they are connected between the computer and the VCR. It is then possible to record the video on your computer's hard disc onto VHS tape. If your camcorder can do this (or you want to check if it can) connect your computer to the camcorder using a FireWire cable and the camera to the VCR using the cable supplied with the camcorder. Now export your video from the computer to the camcorder while keeping an eye on the television.

Remember that if you use this method, or you record via an A to D converter, the computer has no control over the VCR and you will have to start (and stop) the recording at the appropriate point.

Exporting to disc-based media

We use the term 'disc-based media' to cover a wide range of disc formats that use recordable (or rewritable) CDs and DVDs. Disc-based media – in general – are preferred by many users because discs, though liable to scratching and surface damage, are seen as a more resilient medium than videotape. There are also other advantages. Discs are more compact to store, have a longevity (that admittedly has only been proved in accelerated life-cycle experiments) measured in decades and are potentially cheaper per unit. Discs can be designed with tracks and chapters that (like on an audio CD) can make accessing a specific track much swifter than using tape.

DVD is often seen as the only disc-based system and it is true that it offers the best quality and the greatest versatility but is not unique.

In fact there is a range of CD-based formats that includes the VideoCD (VCD), Super VCD and Extra VCD. There is even a CD format that uses the DVD recording regime. Table 5 offers a comparison between these formats, illustrating the quality available and the replay method.

Table 5

Format Name	Compression Format (p.132)	Max. video duration*	Picture Quality**	Disc Type ment	Playback Require-
VideoCD (VCD)	MPEG1	60 minutes	VHS	CD-R CD-RW	Most DVD players, VCD players
SuperVCD	MPEG1 or 2	30 minutes	VHS, SVHS	CD-R CD-RW	Some DVD players
XVCD (ExtraVCD)	MPEG1 or 2	20–40 minutes	VHS, SVHS	CD-R CD-RW	Some DVD players
miniDVD	MPEG2	15 minutes	Broadcast	CD-R CD-RW	Some DVD players
DVD-R	MPEG2	60–120 minutes	Broadcast	DVD-R	Any DVD player

*Maximum duration can depend on picture content, encoding type and data rates.
**Picture quality can vary depending on data rates.

MiniDVD, sometimes called compactDVD or cDVD, offer the opportunity to burn DVD data onto a conventional CD-R or CD-RW disc. Increasingly DVD players are supporting this format but older machines may not. This is because DVD players (which are essentially specialized computer systems) identify the disc type when the disc is loaded and load a corresponding driver. When a miniDVD is loaded CD replay drivers are loaded and there is an immediate digital impasse that results in the disc being rejected.

For our purposes we shall look at the two most widely available (and widely replayable) formats – VideoCD and DVD-R.

VideoCDs offer quality that is usually described as similar to (but never better than) a good VHS video recording, rather than the somewhat better offering of DVD. However, VideoCDs can be produced using standard CD-R or CD-RW drives and replayed on computers, most DVD players and also VideoCD players.

Video compression formats

Before looking in detail at the physical (and virtual) distribution methods for our video let's examine the fundamental video file formats involved and to which our production will need to be converted to make it compatible with computer-based and television-based hardware.

MPEG

Also an acronym for the Motion Picture Experts Group, the term MPEG defines a set of movie image compression techniques devised and monitored by this industry body. The rationale for the several MPEG formats is to convert the enormous data files generated by digital video into files that are significantly more compact, suitable for storage on a disc or even transmission via the Internet. And we need to achieve this compression without unduly compromising the quality of the resultant video.

MPEG1 is the baseline format used for VideoCDs. It rose to prominence (at least as far as the consumer was concerned) in the early 1990s when it was the format chosen for 'full motion video' (i.e. movie replay) on CD-I (CD Interactive) players, a precursor of DVD players. CD-I also enabled the playing of interactive games, while VideoCD enabled a whole movie to be squeezed onto one (or sometimes two) discs.

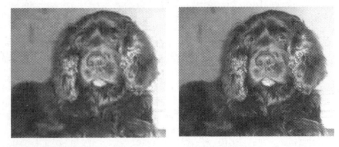

in close-up, MPEG1 (left) compared with the better MPEG2

CD-I did not prove the hit that its progenitors had hoped and languished for some time before quietly disappearing. However, the VideoCD element lived on, largely on account of the popularity of the format in the Far East. In markets where VCR penetration was low and the public appetite for pre-recorded films was greater than that for time-shifting broadcast programming, the enthusiasm continues to this day. Here you will also find dedicated (and low price) VideoCD players and recorders, though the rapid worldwide adoption of DVD as a video format is now driving DVD players – with VideoCD compatibility. Having kept the format alive, it was subsequently readopted more widely as a convenient way of storing consumer digital video.

MPEG2 appeared as the answer to criticisms of MPEG1, in particular the average image quality and limited sound options. Hence MPEG2 video has around four times the resolution and can handle multichannel sound. In practical terms this gives the format about twice the resolution of VHS video.

Of the other MPEG formats (of which there are many) the only one of any importance to us is MPEG4, which is a low bandwidth multimedia format used from Version 6 of Apple's QuickTime (below). It is principally designed to deliver high quality video over the Web.

QuickTime

A format and a technology, QuickTime is used to enable video, audio and image use in a number of applications including the QuickTime Player. It was originally conceived to circumvent the need for a costly hardware playback adaptor. In its early days QuickTime movies featured small (160 × 120 pixel) images replayed at 12 frames per second, less than half that currently used.

QuickTime Pro is a more comprehensive version of the QuickTime Player that permits limited editing and transcoding of media files including those created originally in DV or AVI format. QuickTime can also be used to produce movie files suitable for emailing and Internet use. We look at QuickTime in considerably more detail in the following chapter.

AVI

An acronym for Audio Video Interleave. It is a file format originally devised by Microsoft that handles only audio and video. Files created in AVI format can be replayed using the Windows Media Player, which is provided with copies of Windows and is available as a download for Macintosh users from www.microsoft.com. Microsoft no longer supports AVI, preferring to promote its Windows Media/Direct Show technology. Digital stills cameras that feature a movie mode usually record movies in the AVI format.

Checking a DVD player for VideoCD compatibility

If you are in the market for a DVD player, or have a model already, how can you assess its compatibility with VideoCD discs? There is – I'm afraid – no easy answer. Even if, like most models, the front panel is emblazoned with 'VideoCD Compatible' that is no guarantee that the VideoCDs that you create will work.

The usual advice given is to take a commercial VideoCD, copy it twice, first to a CD-R disc and then to a CD-RW disc. Attempt to play the original and each of the two copies in your DVD player or your shortlist of prospective purchases. You will probably find that most DVD players will play the commercial disc and the CD-RW. DVD players are more tolerant of CD-RW discs compared with CD-R.

Of course, this makes the presumption that you have access to a commercially pressed VideoCD. In the absence of one of these you'll have to follow the procedure outlined here to create a VideoCD and press (or rather, burn) your own copies on CD-R and CD-RW. Alternatively, check out websites for advice (use a search engine to search on VideoCD compatibility to find sites relevant to your own DVD player).

Creating a VideoCD

Here's how we can create a VideoCD using movie footage generated in our applications iMovie and VideoWave. VideoWave provides an option for burning CDs and DVDs from within the application whereas iMovie requires a separate CD burning application (Roxio's Toast is recommended).

Creating a VideoCD with iMovie and Roxio Toast

Producing a movie file from your original movie using Roxio's Toast involves two transcodings of the movie. We first convert it to QuickTime format and then convert this to MPEG1. It is a slow process but not as difficult as the instruction set below may lead you to believe. Roxio Toast 5 Titanium (Mac OS9 and OSX) has been used for the example outlined here.

1   Select File → Export Movie.

2 Choose Export to QuickTime in the dialogue box.

3 In the next dialogue box choose a resolution. As VideoCDs are destined to be played on a TV you can choose the highest setting, Full Quality Large. There is an Expert option provided too. Select this only if you are familiar with the settings involved and have a non-standard application.

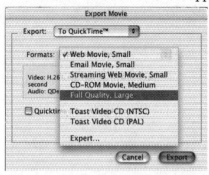

4 Your movie will now be exported in a QuickTime movie format. This transcoding may take a few minutes.

5 Open Toast and Click on the Other button. Choose VideoCD from the pop-up menu. This process will convert our QuickTime movie to the MPEG1 format.

6 Drag the QuickTime movie exported from iMovie to the Toast window.

7 The Toast VideoCD dialogue box opens automatically.

8 Select the video format for the country in which the VideoCD will be replayed (PAL 25fps for UK, Australia and Europe, NTSC 30fps for North America and other countries with the NTSC TV format).

9 Choose an image type: Fit, Crop or Crop and Fit. This determines how your movie will be trimmed if it does not conform to the format of the TV screen.

10 Select a mode. Faster encodes your movie more rapidly but at slightly lower quality; better achieves a better quality but takes longer. Normal, the default setting, is an intermediate setting and good for most purposes.

11 Provide a name for the VideoCD MPEG1 file and press OK. Converting your movie to MPEG1 format can take some time. It is normally suggested that you allow 10 minutes to transcode one minute of original footage; from experience I would suggest this is a little optimistic, but the time will vary according to the speed of your computer. A Progress dialogue box will keep you advised of the progress. Be prepared too for a larger file size. A QuickTime file of 10MB might swell to 60MB (depending on the settings used) when converted to MPEG1.

12 Record this track to a new CD-R or CD-RW. It is recommended that a VideoCD track (or tracks, if you choose to write several VideoCD tracks to the same disc) should be the first tracks on the CD. It is a good idea (to reduce compatibility problems to a minimum) to record only VideoCD tracks on any CD and to write the disc in a single session (multisession recordings are not recommended for VideoCDs).

13 Verify that your recording works in your DVD player and computer.

Note that some, later versions of Toast provide a 'plug-in' to iMovie that makes the conversion process more straightforward. In such cases you will have the option, at step 3 above, to select Toast Video CD (NTSC) or Toast Video CD (PAL) and create an MPEG1 file directly.

Export Movie

Export: [To QuickTime™ ⬦]

Formats: ✓ Web Movie, Small
       Email Movie, Small
Video: H.26   Streaming Web Movie, Small
second   CD-ROM Movie, Medium
Audio: QDe   Full Quality, Large

☐ Quicktir Toast Video CD (NTSC)
        Toast Video CD (PAL)

        Expert...

(Cancel) (Export)

Creating a VideoCD file using VideoWave

VideoWave allows us to publish our movie in a number of different formats by means of a Wizard. We can choose between Windows AVI, MPEG1, MPEG2, DV, Windows Media format or RealNetworks video. For VideoCD production we'll be using MPEG1.

1 Click on the Film Reel icon at the bottom left of the VideoWave interface to open the Produce Movie dialogue box.

2 You can choose to produce the movie from the entire storyline (the default setting and that likely to be used most) or from selected clips.

3 To create a VideoCD select MPEG in the Format drop-down menu. Select VideoCD to produce an NTSC VideoCD or VideoCD – PAL for a PAL version.

4 Click on the Next button when you have entered the appropriate settings.

5 The Summary Page is displayed, giving you a summary of the settings that will be used to produce your video. If you need to make any changes click on the Back button to open the previous dialogue; if the settings are okay, click on Produce to begin the transcoding process. This may take some minutes, depending on the length of the original video.

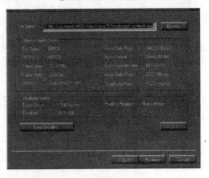

6 The resultant file can be burned onto a CD directly or imported into a CD burning application (such as Roxio's Easy CD Creator).

Creating a VideoCD from within VideoWave

You can also create a VideoCD from within VideoWave, using a process ostensibly developed for DVD creation. This gives you more flexibility than the simple recording of a VideoCD MPEG file and permits the addition of features such as titles and menus.

Begin by clicking on the DVD button on the toolbar. The screen will reformat under the banner 'DVD Authoring'. Then select the VCD button from the New Project Settings dialogue box. An information panel will advise you that this will create a

VideoCD and that the quality of this will be inferior to DVD. From here on, the process is the same as that for creating a DVD or miniDVD, described below.

Publishing to DVD

The renaissance of VideoCD is due in no small part to the enthusiasm whipped up by DVD video not being matched by economic hardware to produce DVDs easily and cheaply in a domestic environment. DVD-R drives, capable of burning DVD video discs, first appeared in commercially available computers in 2000, debuting in selected Macintosh G4 models. But it was not until 2002 when similar drives appeared in Windows machines and (perhaps most significantly) in Apple's consumer level iMacs, that DVD creation became a viable option for the rest of us.

With regard to the use of DVDs as a distribution medium it is interesting to note that the rate of DVD player sales is the highest for any new consumer technology. Though still substantially outnumbered by VCRs, DVD player penetration is increasing fast.

A DVD typically comprises a number (one or more) of video clips that are accessed via a menu. This menu can be hierarchical, that is leads to submenus and sub-submenus. Creating a DVD production involves adding video menus and, perhaps, other subsidiary files and linking them so that a viewer can navigate to each via the menu structure.

Using iMovie and iDVD to create a DVD

Apple's strategy with iMovie is to make movie creation as simple as possible and hence the production of DVDs is not possible from within iMovie. However, Apple have produced iDVD, a similarly simple application that is supplied, free of charge, with all Macintosh computers featuring a DVD-R SuperDrive. As iMovie is effectively a simplified version of Apple's professional video editing application Final Cut Pro so iDVD is an essential version of its DVD authoring application DVD Pro.

Despite there being two applications required to produce a DVD from raw movie footage, this is no real hardship as we will see. The stages involved in DVD creation are:

1 creating and finishing your movie in iMovie
2 exporting the movie in a format recognizable to iDVD
3 importing this movie file into iDVD
4 creating the DVD
5 burning the DVD disc.

Step 4 involves us exploiting the unique virtues of a DVD disc, creating the menus, links and layouts that will be familiar to those already acquainted with DVD videos.

Let's begin the production with a complete iMovie movie.

1 Select File → Export Movie.
2 From the pull-down menu select iDVD. Give your exported file a name and click on Save.
3 Close iMovie and open iDVD. If this is the first time you've used iDVD you'll notice the start screen and many other of the program elements are similar to those of iMovie. To start a new project click on New Project and give the project a name.
4 Once saved the iDVD workspace will open, comprising a workspace window and control buttons below this. To the left are the Theme, Folder and Slideshow buttons; to the right the Disc space used/free indicator, Preview button and Disc Burn button.

5 Begin by setting a Theme. The Theme is a set of DVD movie interface elements that gives the production its look. It comprises background and menu graphics. A range of themes are provided that you can scroll through. Click on the Theme button to display these. If you wish you can customize any of the standard themes to:
• import an image from your hard disc
• create Title graphics using any text, style, colour or size

- choose or alter the button sizes or shapes used
- alter the labelling style and position
- save your custom style for future use.

6 Add video material. iDVD permits the inclusion of either video footage or still images, presented as slideshows. There is no distinction made when viewing these; clicking on a button will display the associated visuals whether video or images. To add a video clip choose Select File → Import Video and select your video clip (alternatively you can drag the video clip file from the finder to the iDVD screen). Video clips are displayed as thumbnails when dragged to the iDVD window; you can alter the thumbnail by selecting it and moving the bar above the thumbnail to an appropriate position.

7 Adding a slideshow requires the slideshow to be built first. As it is outside the scope of this book, refer to the online help provided with iDVD.

8 Add a folder. Up to six elements (typically video clips) can be added to a menu. If you require more, use folders, each of which allows a further six items to be stored in a submenu. Click on the Folder button to create a new folder and add new elements as outlined in step 6.

9 Test your production. Press the Preview button and play your DVD using the surrogate remote control that appears. You can navigate the production in the same way as you will be able to with the finished result, so this is a good opportunity to 'debug' and check the production for errors. Click on the Preview button again to return and make any necessary changes.

10 Burn the DVD. Though you've tested your DVD in real time, encoding it to burn on a DVD and the burning itself will take some time. As a rule of thumb it will take about four times the total duration of the video material provided. Hence if you use the maximum play time permitted of 90 minutes, prepare to wait six hours! In practice this time will be affected by the speed of your computer, the type of processor and the type of content provided. No matter what, though, it never seems to burn in less time ...

Using VideoWave to create a DVD

As we alluded to earlier when creating VideoCDs, DVDs can be produced from within VideoWave. As we'll see the process is very similar to that for creating a VideoCD though ultimately we will have much more freedom in final production. Note that this facility is only available from VideoWave version 5.

1 Click on the DVD button on the toolbar and wait for the DVD Authoring desktop to appear.

2 When the New Project Settings dialogue box appears select the DVD button (alternately select the miniDVD button if you intend to produce a miniDVD). Click OK.

3 The DVD Authoring desktop contains a new toolbar to the left with DVD authoring-specific tools. In sequence these are, from the top: Add Backgrounds, Add Video, Add Buttons, Change Text, Add Audio, Preview (project) and Return to Editing. The Filmreel button at the base of the toolbar is now indicated by a DVD. Press this to burn your production.

4 Click on the Background Pictures button to give your menus an appropriate background. A wide range of abstract and pictorial backgrounds are provided but you can also use one of your own images.

5 Add video clips to the DVD by clicking on the Add Video button, then drag the appropriate clips from the Library to the monitor window. A thumbnail of the clip will appear in the window and you can use the slider to move through the clip to get alternate thumbnails. Choose the thumbnail that best represents your clip.

6 Click on the Buttons button to alter the frame of the video clip. Note that you can resize and reposition the thumbnail and frame by dragging on the handles around the frame.

7 Change the text font settings by first clicking on the Text button and dragging a text style to the text in the monitor window. You can rename the thumbnail (which by default adopts the name of the original video clip) by clicking on the text.

8 Add further video clips by repeating steps 4 to 7 above.

9 You can also add (or delete) menus by clicking on the Menus tab on the menubar across the top of the screen.

10 Now divide clips, if you wish, into chapters (the DVD equivalent to tracks). This makes it easy to navigate to a precise point in the production. Highlight the clip to be divided in the menubar (ensure that the Titles tab is pressed to display the clips) and then press the Add Chapters button. This is the icon to the left of the first clip.

11 A dialogue box will open displaying a small monitor window at the top. Divide into chapters by using the slider to move through the clip and clicking the Add button at each point you want a chapter break added. Note that dividing a clip into chapters does not physically divide it nor does it interrupt the replay of the clip; chapters are a purely navigational tool.

12 You are now ready to burn your DVD (or CD in the case of a miniDVD). Click on the Burn button. A wizard will guide you through making the appropriate settings (such as television format and write speed).

Creating DVDs using CD burning applications

There's no need to use dedicated applications for DVD video to burn your DVD. Once you have created your DVD project (in iDVD, VideoWave or any other comparable application) you can use a disc-burning application to create the disc. Even when, like VideoWave and iDVD, you can burn your production from within the application, this can often be a more speedy way of producing your disc.

In a burning application such as Toast, configuring to burn a DVD is very similar to creating a CD.

1 Select the Other button from the interface and hold down the mouse button.

2 Select DVD from the pop-up menu.

3 Drag the folder containing the DVD content and associated files to the window. Unless you have changed the name of the folder this will be called VIDEO_TS.
4 Insert a blank DVD-R and click the Record button followed by Write Disc in the dialogue box that opens.

Commericial DVD discs

The DVD-R discs used to create our DVD videos are not identical to those used for commercial pressings. Writing processes apart (commercial discs are stamped rather than burned), a commercial disc is dual layered, featuring a semi-transparent top layer and reflective lower layer. By altering the laser focusing each layer can be distinguished uniquely and read without interference from the other. This gives the disc a capacity of nearly 8 Gbytes, sufficient for a movie, titles and some 'bonus features'. Discs to this standard are known as DVD-9, the single layer DVD-R discs, DVD-5. Even greater capacities are possible using double-sided discs. Virtually every DVD-R drive is designed only to burn single layer DVDs.

Commercial DVDs also include copy protection (usually Macrovision), which disrupts the copying process, rendering copies of poor, often unwatchable quality. They will often (other than in the case of exempt titles) contain a Region Code. This controversial addition prevents discs produced for the market in one region being played in players in another, for copyright and licensing purposes. The discs you will create will contain neither of these safeguards, though whether they would be of any value to our domestic productions is debatable.

Writing to a DLT tape

DLT (Digital Linear Tape) tape is a commonly available tape medium often used for backing up large hard discs. The tape is also that used if you are sending your DVD production to a production house for commercial DVD production. You might use a production house if you need to produce a number of copies of a DVD or to produce a DVD with a larger duration than the single-sided single-layer discs will permit.

Applications such as Toast will write directly to a DLT drive and on to DLT tape. The recording will be in a format that the production house can use to cut a master – and copies – of, say, a DVD9 format disc.

10

QuickTime and Web movie publishing

In this chapter you will learn

- about QuickTime
- how to create streamed video
- how to broadcast on the Internet.

Technologies including QuickTime have given us the opportunity to broaden our movie publishing horizons to include the Internet. To conclude our discussion of movie publishing we'll take a look at this and other similar Web movie technologies and also examine the possibilities of video streaming.

QuickTime has long been an important part of Web publishing but is not just limited to Internet applications. Though it is both a piece of software and a file format it is probably more appropriate to describe it as a facilitating technology. In more simple English this means it can facilitate multimedia features (images, audio and animation in addition to video) in other software applications. We can exploit the tools and the technology to create elements for our movies and to export our movies in novel ways.

The software component of QuickTime is most clearly seen as the QuickTime Player, a movie player that uses a simple interface similar to that of the monitor window in iMovie or VideoWave to display a movie and provide playback controls for the user. QuickTime – and the QuickTime player – are often regarded as Macintosh applications as they form a fundamental element of that computer's operating system (and are used by default for multimedia presentations on that platform). However, QuickTime is also available for Windows and UNIX operating systems, as a free download from the Apple website.

QuickTime movies

The power of QuickTime over other video or multimedia technologies is its ability to support the greatest range of media file formats. It also works equally well for Internet-based applications as it does for those that are computer or CD-ROM based and, as we've already mentioned, features cross platform support for Windows and Mac operating systems. For our purposes here it is important to note that QuickTime will handle all the important formats that are used for video and also those used for components – such as sound and images – that might be incorporated in our movie production (see Table 6). Though it is only of peripheral importance to the movie maker, QuickTime also permits the creation of immersive environments, known as QuickTime VR (Virtual Reality). These are based on still images but give the viewer the opportunity to move around a 360-degree panorama and even zoom in or out on selected items.

Table 6 QuickTime media formats

AIFF	MP3
Audio CD	MPEG1
AVI	MPEG4 (from version 6)
BMP	Photoshop
DV	PICT
GIF (and Animated GIF)	PNG
JPEG	QuickTime Image
Macromedia Flash	TIFF
MIDI	WAV

Note: This is not an exhaustive list of media formats compatible with QuickTime.

QuickTime Pro

The QuickTime Player is an excellent resource that enables the display or playing of a great range of media file formats but remains essentially a player for these media files. To edit and manipulate them we need to use the 'Pro' version.

grab sliders are the visible difference between QuickTime Pro (here) and the standard version

This extended functionality comes at a modest cost (around US$30) and can be purchased from the Apple QuickTime (www.apple.com/quicktime) website. In fact, if you have QuickTime installed on your computer you will also have QuickTime Pro; for your payment you'll be given an unlock key to unlock the extra functionality.

With QuickTime Pro we can, in addition to the simple viewing and playing of media files:

1 Save and Export movies created in alternate formats as DV movies (which can be imported into iMovie or other applications).
2 Edit movie clips prior to inclusion in our movie-making application.
3 Download and save QuickTime-based movies and resources from the Web.
4 Convert media into a form that can be used in our movie application.
5 Export movies to QuickTime for subsequent delivery on CD-ROM or via the Internet.

The last option provides us with the means to export files to a wide range of destinations. For example, the export settings provided by iMovie for QuickTime movies are:

1 Email Movie, Small: This is the smallest movie setting that is still capable of producing a recognizable image. Accompanied by mono sound the image window will be very small (160 × 120 pixels), blocky and jerky, but the filesize will be small enough to allow for easy emailing. A check box enables the video to be made compatible with the older, Version 3 of QuickTime. Check this box if your intended recipients might have this.
2 Web Movie, Small: Slightly larger both in screen size (240 × 180 pixels) and file size, this setting adds stereo sound but is still small enough to be downloaded using conventional modems (i.e. not ISDN or broadband).
3 Streaming Web Movie, Small: Creates a movie file suitable for streaming video when uploaded to an appropriate streaming video website. See below for further details on streaming video.
4 CD-ROM Movie, Medium: At 320 × 240 pixels and with 15 frames per second this option provides a good quality movie for replaying from CD-ROM. Image quality will be quite acceptable for multimedia presentations but is still far short of television quality.
5 Full Quality, Large: The option we used for generating material to be incorporated on a VideoCD, the 720 × 480 pixel movies feature full frame rates (appropriate to the PAL or NTSC requirement) and high bit-rate stereo sound.

6 Expert: There's little need to use this for most applications; it is designed for making custom settings for non-standard movie requirements.

If you have Roxio's Toast installed you may also see the two options (detailed on p.134) for making VideoCDs directly from iMovie.

Streaming video

Distributing your movies by email is neither the most efficient use of the Web nor the method most likely to endear you to your recipients. If your movie is compressed enough to comprise a small file the quality will probably be too poor to be enjoyed; any larger and users of metered telephone lines will be reaching for the disconnect button.

Streaming offers an alternative that can result in much more satisfactory performance. Though it is a more complex technology, if you intend to best exploit Web distribution it could be a very important medium. And as increasing numbers of users gain broadband Internet connections along with unmetered Internet access, it is becoming an increasingly viable publishing medium.

The mechanics of streaming

Streamed video is widespread across the Web. If you have ever visited the BBCi website (www.bbc.co.uk), for example, you'll have had the opportunity to enjoy news stories and even complete news programmes as streamed video. In doing so you may have been requested to download the special player software (in this case RealPlayer) required to play the video.

Video streaming works by downloading the movie file from a file server to a recipient's player software using an Internet connection much the same as that used to download emails. Streaming differs from emailing in that a streamed file can be played prior to complete download. Hence once sufficient data is received to play the movie, it can be played by the viewer. Downloading of the remaining part of the file continues.

Once a file server and the user's player have established contact a complex handshaking procedure begins. This ensures that the data file being delivered is appropriate (in terms of file size and download speed) for the user's player and also maintains a buffer of data sufficient to allow for download problems. Should data not be sent correctly then it can be re-sent without interrupting the programme flow as seen by the viewer.

The rate of streaming and, consequently, the quality of video received is very dependent on the Internet connection. If you have a standard modem connection (that will manage only 56Kbps on a good day) then the quality of the video received will be less than that possible using ISDN, ADSL, DSL or a faster bandwidth. File servers can determine the optimum connection speeds and send the appropriate data stream.

Streaming technologies

Three discrete technologies are used for streaming video and it probably comes as no surprise to learn that they are incompatible with each other. These are QuickTime, Windows Media and Real. On a positive note the players for each are freely available for each of the principal computing platforms.

QuickTime

Apple introduced streaming technology with QuickTime Version 4. Exploiting the streaming capabilities of QuickTime requires a video editing application that supports streaming output. Fortunately (for Macintosh users at least) iMovie is a video editor that is capable of producing streaming-compliant QuickTime files. You can also use QuickTime Pro to produce files within the QuickTime environment. See www.apple.com/quicktime for more information.

Windows Media

Microsoft's Windows Media offers Intelligent Streaming, a mechanism that produces output files that are matched to the connection speed and bandwidth of the user's Internet connection. Usefully this requires that only a single file need be created and separate (different bandwidth) tracks attached. Creating a Windows Media file requires the PC only Windows Media encoder. Details are available from the Microsoft website, www.microsoft.com/windows/windowsmedia.

Real

Real (sometimes called RealSystem) is a product of RealNetworks. An important feature of the Real streaming technology is the support of synchronized multimedia integration language (SMIL) that enables the easy embedding of Real Streaming video within Web pages. Real not only offers a free player for download but also a free (if basic) encoding application, RealProducer. There is a more comprehensive product, Producer Plus, that can be purchased at Real's website, www.real.com.

Creating streamable video

Though streaming is purely a video delivery medium, the nature of that medium puts some restrictions (which are recommended rather than obligatory) on the material we can use. Though sometimes seen as compromises, these limitations are suggested to make the streamed production more watchable given the confines of the delivery system. Here are the principal ones:

• Text: Use large text sizes, simple sans serif fonts (such as Arial) and as few words as possible. Some proponents of streaming video suggest that you use no text at all as low bandwidth reproduction is very poor indeed. Substituting voice overs and more detailed narration is often a good way to avoid titles.

• Sound: Sound is even more important on a streamed video as its quality will not be perceived to drop as much as the video when the movie files are heavily compressed.

• Use close-ups: Sweeping landscapes, crowd scenes and other elements opitimized in widescreen movie productions do not successfully transfer to streaming video and tend to be represented as indistinct blurs. Use the techniques employed by TV (rather than film) and feature close ups of people or objects that are important to the scene.

• Simple works best: In a similar vein, simple scenes and scenery are not only easier to view, they also make for more easily compressed files. The algorithm that compresses the video is more successful in handling simple scenes than it is with more complex ones.

• Image size and quality: Both are determining factors for how effective streaming will be. It is a good idea to test your production by producing some comparison footage in which the window size, quality and frame rate (i.e. the number of frames per second) are varied. For example, you may find that a lower frame rate, may give a better overall effect, permitting larger or sharper individual frames.

The process of producing a movie for streaming is less contentious and involves:

1 creating a movie using any video editor
2 saving the movie in a format suitable for streaming
3 uploading to a website or streaming server.

If this movie is one that you will be distributing using other media too (such as on DVD or videotape) ensure that you also make a copy at the highest quality. If you save only in the format required for streaming the quality will not be sufficient for other purposes.

The video editing applications we have discussed here are ideal for producing video for streaming. You can use VideoWave to produce material to be streamed using Windows Media or Real; iMovie is ideal for QuickTime. As we mentioned earlier you could use the free application RealProducer to produce a Real streaming video file from an iMovie original.

Configuring a movie for Internet streaming

The simplest tool for creating a movie suitable for streaming is the QuickTime Pro player. The basic requirement is that your video is compressed to a degree suitable for the bandwidth you intend to use for the streaming. Though the following applies to QuickTime Pro, you'll need to make similar settings when preparing a movie using any preparative application.

1 Open the QuickTime Player
2 Select File menu ➜ Export
3 Choose Movie to QuickTime Movie from the pop-up menu
4 Select a Streaming Option. Note that HTTP streaming movies are designed to work with any Web server and that the RTSP streaming format is designed for QuickTime Streaming Servers.

Uploading your video file is, in principal, as easy as uploading any other file or media to a website. But there are special considerations to be taken into account. You'll need to check that your proposed destination will accept (and permit the replay of) streaming media and, if so, that the bandwidths are appropriate. Contact your Internet Service Provider (ISP) or check their Help or FAQ pages to see if your production can be accommodated.

Fast Start movies

QuickTime also permits you to watch movies as the original files are downloaded from conventional HTTP or FTP transfer protocols. This is not streaming in the true sense of the word but a process known as Fast Start. It is often more acceptable to the recipients of a movie to use Fast Start than to rely on their patience, waiting for the movie to download in full.

Fast Start enables viewers to download a movie at the highest speed their particular connection will allow. Once a proportion of the file (10 or 20 per cent, typically) is downloaded replay begins. If the replay catches up with the downloaded percentage, replay is paused but can be restarted (either from the current point or the beginning) manually.

Using Fast Start requires no special streaming software, but does require that the movie is stored as a Fast Start file (which can be done using QuickTime Pro player). The benefits include movie delivery being independent of the connection speed and the possibility of delivering alternate file types including virtual reality files. To the viewer a Fast Start movie also looks like a streamed video.

The drawback of Fast Start is that the file is downloaded to the recipient's computer. While this means that they can replay it as often as possible and even save it on to their hard disc or CD, it also means that copies of your valuable source material could be circulating outside your control.

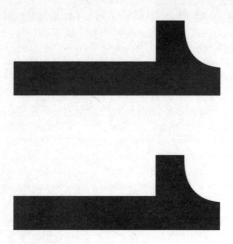

11

digitizing video and automated production

In this chapter you will learn:
- about converting analogue video to digital
- creating a movie with VideoImpression®
- Using Cinematic for automated video production.

Let us look more closely at two techniques that can extend your video production capabilities. First we'll look at a simple method of including analogue video footage in productions. This is ideal (if not essential) if you need to add archive material to your current productions. The second is automated movie production. Though no software can create a finished movie from your rough footage (and would not be able to interpret our creative vision, in any case) some products can do much of the mechanical cutting, trimming and fitting. We'll see how effective these are and where they are best used.

Creating digital video from existing analogue sources

We've mentioned at several points in this book the question of using analogue video in your productions, either as the extant source material or to integrate in productions that principally feature digital video. We've looked too at the use of A to D converters such as the Hollywood Bridge and Formac Studio.

Let's now look at an alternate system that is ideal if you want to digitize your analogue back catalogue of video footage but can't justify a full-blown A to D conversion system. This system comes to us thanks to USB, the increasingly ubiquitous PC connection systems.

USB capture device

USB Digitizers often come with software not only to effect the transfer of material but also to edit the transferred footage. Though the supplied applications vary, a commonly offered editing application is VideoImpression from ArcSoft. It is available for both Windows PCs and Macintoshes and can also be purchased and downloaded from the ArcSoft website. We'll use this here because it is simple and effective for both downloading and editing.

Installing your USB Digitizer

The USB digitizing package will comprise the USB digitizer itself, software and (though not in all cases) the appropriate cabling to connect the digitizer to the computer and the video source. The computer connection comprises a simple A–B-type USB lead whose connectors are unambiguous. Those provided for connection to the video source (which may be an analogue VCR or analogue camcorder) usually comprise three phono connectors. Colour coded yellow, white and red, these are for the inputs of the video signal and right and left sound tracks respectively.

To effect a connection to a VCR you may need a phono to phono connecting lead (that links the connectors on the digitizer with the corresponding ones on the VCR) or SCART to phono. In the latter case you need to ensure that the phono plugs deliver a video-out signal from the VCR. Two-way cables (that provide three phono inputs and three phono outputs, or switchable input/output phono cables) are often a better investment and will enable recording back to the VCR if required.

Install the software. This will usually comprise driver software for the digitizer and editing software (which also handles the import of the video footage) as we described above.

Capturing video

With the hardware connected and the software installed you are all set to begin capturing video. Start by launching the software, in this case VideoImpression.

1 Start a new project by clicking on the New button on the start screen.

2 Choose New Album from the drop-down menu at the top of the new project screen and give the project a meaningful name such as Analogue Capture.

3 Click on the Acquire button, indicated by the camcorder icon.

4 With the capture window displayed, click on the Video Setting button. You can make changes to the settings with regard to how the video is captured but in most cases (and certainly where this software has been provided with a digitizer) you can leave the default settings. You might like to alter the settings later, following your first acquisition, to see if you can improve on the quality or to alter frame or quality settings if the digitizer is having problems providing acceptable quality using the defaults.

5 Choose a Source. This will be your USB digitizer. Click on OK to return to the capture window.

6 Select a Video Size. Larger frame sizes are better but will require more powerful processing; again it is probably best to leave this at its default setting. If it is clear that your processor is struggling to digitize at the set video size you can return later and set a smaller size. Conversely, if your computer is having no problems you might like to increase the size. Click OK to accept the default setting or after you have made any changes.

7 Configure the sound in the same way. Choose a sound input source. If your VCR (or camcorder) is running and replaying a tape you will be able to hear this now on your computer. It is a good idea to have a tape running so that you can make any necessary changes to the volume and the gain (amplification).

8 Begin capturing your video. Rewind your source videotape to just before the footage you want to import (this will give you the opportunity to cue the footage). Start the VCR playing then click on Video Capture at the point you want to start capturing. This is an instantaneous process so you can press the Capture button at the exact point you want to begin capture. At the end, click Stop Capture. The clip will be added to the Album and a thumbnail shown in the Album window.

9 You can now repeat for any additional clips you want to capture.

Now, with your video clips acquired and digitized, you can use them in your favourite movie editing application or you can compile a movie from within VideoImpression. From VideoImpression you can export in MPEG1, MOV or AVI format.

Producing a movie using VideoImpression

If you choose to use VideoImpression to create movies from your digitized footage, you'll find it an easy way to produce a compilation. Not as comprehensive as VideoWave or even iMovie it is nonetheless a great package for assembling and editing your converted video clips. You can even use VideoImpression to quickly produce your rough cut and then import the resultant footage into a more heavyweight application for further editing. We make the presumption here that you have captured some video clips from an analogue source and have them collected as an album.

1 Open your Album (from the VideoImpression front page click on New and then select the album in which your clips were saved from the drop-down menu). Your clips are displayed as thumbnails, in the order you collected them. Note the storyboard, shown as a filmstrip metaphor, along the base of the screen. This comprises spaces for the video clips, transitions (between the video clip windows) and has two soundtracks ranged along the bottom.

2 Click on a clip thumbnail to highlight it. To place this in the first available position double click on it, or drag it to the space.

3 Repeat for subsequent clips.

4 To apply a transitional effect click on the edit button, just above the storyboard and then click on the Transitions button. Choose a transition. Depending on the transition selected you can vary the duration of the transition or other parameters (such as fade rates) from the dialogue boxes that appear. Note that the transition is applied between your currently selected clip and the previous.

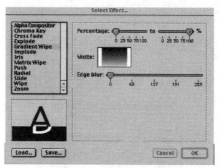

5 To add text (such as a title, or a caption) click on the Text icon.
A text box will appear on the currently selected clip. Enter your
text, using the buttons beneath the monitor window to change
the text size, font and duration displayed. Use the Title Effect
button to vary the way the text is shown (you can choose
between effects such as static (default) fade in, drop down,
rotate and so on. You can also use the drag handles on the text
box to reposition the text anywhere on the screen.

Viewing and saving a VideoImpression movie

When your video has been compiled (or partially compiled) you
can view the results.

1 Click on the Play Movie icon.
2 The View Screen appears and you can watch your movie by
pressing the Play button beneath the monitor window.

3 If you are happy with the results and have finished compiling,
click on the Save button to save the results. The save option
provides a succinct list of options. Those important to us
include:

- Save Movie to AVI format
- Save Movie to DV Stream
- Save Movie to QuickTime Movie
- Save Movie to VideoCD.

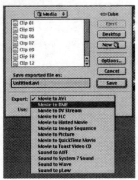

4 You can also select a TV format, choosing between PAL, NTSC or Custom.

5 Save your movie. This can take a few minutes, after which you will be asked to specify a location for your stored movie (it will be placed in VideoImpression's Album folder by default).

6 If you were not happy with the results you can press the Edit button to return to the Edit Screen and make any changes that you require.

VideoImpression allows you to add image and sound files to your production and to add coloured backgrounds to your titles. Should you wish to add additional sound files (for background music, for example) you can do so and even edit these.

Automated production using Cinematic

Cinematic's interface and operations have much in common with VideoWave – predictably, perhaps, as both hail from the same software house – but it is designed as a more automated product, making it ideal both for those with less experience of movie making and those who need a more expedient way of producing movies.

Note that Cinematic is available only for Windows. Also it is not recommended that Cinematic and VideoWave are both installed on the same computer. There are some conflicting configurations that could affect one or other of the applications if installed concurrently.

Cinematic works on three broad levels. The level you might choose will depend upon the requirements for your current project.

• CineMagic: Using the CineMagic option your video clips and audio tracks are automatically compiled to produce a finished movie with the minimum of user intervention. Movies are produced according to stylistic guidelines (templates) that determine the mood; you can choose from styles such as pop video or old-time movie. Clips are organized and transitions added automatically.

• StoryBuilder: If you require more directorial control but still want to produce a movie quickly, StoryBuilder is ideal. Again you can specify a style template but a wizard then requests further information prior to producing a structured storyboard automatically.

• On Your Own: Using an environment that is broadly similar to that of VideoWave the freeform working option gives you the same creative freedom of the sibling product. This option can also be used to modify or refine a production that has been created in CineMagic or StoryBuilder modes.

Using Cinematic's CineMagic option

Here's an indication of how easy the use of the totally automatic CineMagic option is in movie creation – and the limitations that can be imposed. In particular, CineMagic will trim video clips to fit the length of the audio track provided rather than fitting the music to the visuals. It is therefore important that the video material provided is substantially longer than any audio track (twice the length is suggested).

1 Click on the CineMagic icon on the Welcome screen.

2 Select your video clips from the Library (the Library here has the same purpose as that of VideoWave) by dragging them, in your required sequence, to the panel below the monitor window. Each clip will be listed along with a corresponding thumbnail.

3 Press the Next button when all required clips are listed. The Audio Window will appear, enabling audio clips to be added. You can drag these in the same way as the video clips. Note the point we made above. Any audio tracks you provide must be around half the length of the video material already added.

4 Now choose a style template for the production. This will determine not only the visual style but the tempo to which the movie is compiled. It is unlikely that the limited list of templates will provide for all eventualities, but choose that closest to your production. For example, the selection Personal is suitable for all movies in which people are the principal elements; the movie will be cut with a bias towards retaining footage of people.

5 Press Next to launch the Analyzer. When this begins Cinematic will start analysing the footage and audio that you have provided and interpreting it in the style that you have suggested. This may take some time but the indicator bar will display progress and the files being analysed are shown below.

6 On completion of the analysis click on the Play button to play the movie that has been created for you. If you like it, save it. If not you can edit it further by clicking on the 'I want to edit my Production' button.

Users with even a little experience of video editing are likely to be put off by the limited intervention provided with CineMagic. In fact, the system works very well and is ideal for producing a rough edit. Most users are likely to choose the option provided at the end for further editing.

Using the StoryBuilder

Adding some creative control, the StoryBuilder also includes step-by-step guidance. The StoryBuilder divides the movie into three parts: Introduction, Main (the body of the movie) and Ending. You can choose separate styles for each part.

1 Begin a StoryBuilder-controlled production by clicking on the StoryBuilder icon on the Welcome screen.

2 Use the Import Video Clips button to import video clips into the Library (you can select multiple clips by using the control or shift keys when making the selection).

3 Select a template for the video production (themes provided include 'Business', 'Christmas', 'Baby's First Steps' and more). You can capture new video at this point by clicking on the Get button and following the ensuing instructions. Click the Next button when you are ready to continue.

4 We can now create the Introduction. Select a style for the introduction from the drop-down menu. Press the Play button to load the selected style and then Play to preview it. If the style you have chosen is not appropriate you can return and select another.

5 Add any video clips that you wish to use as part of the introduction (the order of clips in the list can be altered by using the up and down arrows). You can regard this list as a basic (and vertically arranged) storyboard.

6 Click Play to load the elements of the introduction and play the introductory passage. If you are happy with your work, press the Next button to continue.

7 Select a style now for the Main part of the movie. Repeat the process above for this section.

8 Press the Next button to add a music track for the main section. A range of resources is provided with Cinematic but you can incorporate your own material (saved as WAV files). Press Next again when you have made your selection.

9 Choose the video clips from the Library for the main section. As in the introductory section you can re-order your selections using the arrow keys.

10 You can also add graphics or animations to the main section. Press the Next button again and make a selection (this is optional). Once you have made a selection, or if you do not want to add either graphics or animation, press Next.

11 We can now compile the Ending section. The process here is very similar to that which we've employed for the Introduction and Main sections. Follow the onscreen instructions, importing media as before.

12 The final stage is production. Here, as with CineMagic, we can choose between exporting the production (in a range of formats) or editing the production further.

Using Cinematic in work on your own mode

We shall not go into the detail here of this mode as it is very similar to that of VideoWave, apart from interface differences.

12 camcorder basics

In this chapter you will learn:
- the basic handling technique of your camcorder
- how to get the best results
- about looking after your camcorder.

Given how easy it is to operate a camcorder it is quite feasible to use one straight from the box. Assuming you've a fully charged battery and appropriate videotape there's no reason not to start collecting footage straight away. Yet spend a few minutes getting familiar with the camcorder first and you – and it – can have a much more meaningful partnership. In this chapter we've distilled some of the operational essentials to speed up the process.

The camera tour

If you are new to videophotography the first time you hold a digital camcorder can be a daunting experience. Almost every part of the surface seems covered with buttons or flaps that open to reveal – well, more buttons. You can forget your angst because many of these buttons are, for taking basic shots, superfluous. Let's do a quick survey of the camera controls – a quick reference for the inexperienced and a reminder to old hacks.

Tape chamber

The compartment for the tape is usually on the side of the camera or sometimes on the base. Press (or push) the button marked eject and the compartment cover will open. Then there will be a few seconds of whirring and grinding. Though it sounds worrying this is perfectly normal. The tape carrier itself will then spring out from the camera ready to accept the tape. Slide in a tape and close the carrier flap. Do take particular notice of any warnings on the tape transport components – depending on model you'll see 'Press Here to Close' or 'Do Not Push Here'. Heed these to prevent any damage. Be mindful, too, that if you have to press anything really hard then something is amiss. All operations should be activated with the lightest of touches and pushes. If all else fails resort to checking in the manual.

one of the few instructions you must obey!

Once the tape is in the carrier and you have pressed the appropriate place the whirring will begin again and the mechanism will return into the camera. Close the outer flap and you are ready to go.

Power up

Fresh out of the box your new camcorder will have a battery that is unlikely to be fully charged. A small residual charge may give the impression of power but it won't last long. Though modern batteries are much more tolerant of intermittent charging it makes good sense to follow the instructions and give the battery a good full charge the first time it is used. This may be a long process (perhaps eight hours, in some cases overnight) but you can be assured that the first time you use it it'll be fully powered.

Do be aware that the batteries provided with cameras are rarely the most powerful (in endurance terms) available. It makes sense to have a second battery and this should be one with greater capacity. You can then keep the original as back-up and enjoy substantially longer shooting times. Note, too, that many cameras will work directly from an AC mains source. It's good to remember this when working at home or elsewhere indoors – you'll not only save on battery power consumption but could be recharging your batteries at the same time!

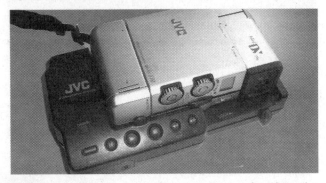

supplied with some models and available as an accessory for others, the docking station makes recharging a cinch

Mode selector

By design the most obvious control is the mode selector. This switches the camera on and between Camera and VCR modes. On some models there may be additional specialist modes, such as photo or memory.

Camera mode lets you record footage (that is, behave as a camera). In this mode the electronic viewfinder and/or LCD panel will be relaying 'live' images from the camera lens and CCD (if the screens are blank it's probably because the lens cap is on). When you press the record button you'll be able to record these views.

The record button is usually quite prominent, often coloured red (though where stylists have had more of a say over the ergonomicists, it could well be bright chrome) and invariably falls under the right thumb. In many cases it's the centre button of the mode selector, which conveniently allows you to select the record mode and control recording using only your thumb. Press it to start recording, press it again to stop.

In VCR mode the recorded footage can be played back using the camera as a videocassette recorder. When set to this mode a group of controls known as video transport controls become active. You'll probably find these near the LCD panel or on the camera side. Rather like those on a conventional videocassette recorder these will enable you to play your tape, cue and review footage.

A note to the left handed: if – like me – you do absolutely everything with your left hand it can be a little disconcerting to find that all camcorders are designed for right-hand operation. There is no easy way (other than when the camera is tripod mounted) to use it left-handed. Don't be too concerned, however. It takes little practice to become quite proficient at using your right thumb. So being left handed should never be an excuse for getting poor results!

the mode selector

Viewing

Your camera may sport a conventional viewfinder, an LCD panel or both.

Viewfinders have taken a back seat to the LCD panel but are excellent for viewing a scene in bright daylight when LCD panels usually get washed out. Increasingly viewfinder images are in colour and – considering how small the LCD panel contained within is – offer surprisingly good image quality. You can adjust the focus of the viewfinder to accommodate variations in eyesight.

LCD panels debuted in analogue models as a replacement for the traditional viewfinder although it is common now to find both provided. The chief benefit of the LCD panel – which typically folds out from the side of the camera – is to allow a greater range of camera positions and convenient viewing. You can hold the camera over your head (ideal in crowd situations)

the viewfinder

or place the camera on the floor and be confident that you are recording the right scene. Just try doing either with the viewfinder! However, the LCD panel has two drawbacks – as we've already mentioned they do not work well in bright sunlight, and their power consumption is somewhat greater than that of a viewfinder LCD.

Zooming

In conventional designs you'll probably discover that if the mode selector and record buttons are under your thumb, the zoom control – which is a rocker switch – is usually under your index finger. Most are pressure sensitive. Press hard forward and it will zoom in fast, use lighter pressure and the zoom speed will be somewhat slower.

It is now almost universal that camcorders include real optical zooms and digital zooms. You'll find that as you zoom in and out the degree of zooming will be shown (usually as an arrow on a bar) on the LCD or viewfinder display. This display will also distinguish the optical and digital zoom ratios.

Viewfinder data

As well as zoom information (which usually appears only when the zoom lens is being operated) your viewfinder or LCD panel will also display other data. At times the screen can be full of information but the good news is that none of this is normally recorded on the videotape. Depending on the mode selected you'll see a clock display (showing current time, or time of recording), battery status, any special modes selected (such as mono or stereo sound) and timecode. Looking like a recording duration counter this identifies every frame in your movie and is a great boon to making frame-accurate edits.

Because there are so many features packed into your video camera, many of the control buttons actually display menus on the screen. Pressing Effects for example may give a menu of effects that you can scroll through (perhaps by using the zoom rocker, in another of its modes) and pressing the record button to make a selection.

Because data is recorded along with your video footage it is important to ensure that the camera is always set to the correct time and date. Many cameras include a small button cell battery, which provides back-up for the date and time.

Care and attention

As you'll see when you open the camera to insert a tape there is an awful lot of electronics and a fair number of mechanical components crammed into a very small space. Reliablity, though, is high so despite the comparatively expensive prices you should expect the camera to perform well for a considerable time. But how can you make those expectations meet reality? Here are a few suggestions on how to make your camera last. Let's get the obvious out of the way first. Camcorders and videotape don't like:

- heat
- direct sunlight
- damp
- high humidity
- dust, sand and other particulates such as smoke
- magnetic fields (including those generated by CRT computer monitors and speakers)
- sharp physical shocks.

Rather than becoming obsessed with these enemies, let common sense prevail. Keeping your camera in a good camera bag will protect it from shocks, dust ingress and, subject to the ambient conditions, head and humidity. It you really want to take the camera on the beach or ski slope, investigate dust covers and dust bags. Like heavy duty plastic bags (but with an optically clear window for the lens) these can save you from the worst of the elements without compromising the handling.

Videotape

Many early VHS videocassette recorders were badly damaged by the use of videotapes that actually contained computer-grade tape. Though this tape was equivalent in quality to that used for video recording it featured different lubricants and different frictional coefficients. The result was very rapid wear and clogging of video heads.

Fortunately digital video tapes are produced by a handful of manufacturers all of whom keep very closely to the specification of the digital video formats. Even so there are slight differences in some of the lubricants used that could – and we can only say could – cause problems if tapes from different brands are used interchangeably. Sticking to one brand lessens the chances of problems through incompatible lubricants mixing.

Lenses

After the tape heads the lens is the most delicate part of your camcorder. Unlike your tape heads it tends to be exposed for much of the time. Conventional wisdom states that you should keep the lens cap on at all times when you are not using the camera either to record a scene or prepare to record.

You'll find that many intensive users eschew this advice and keep the lens cap off pretty well permanently. Lest you should think this utter folly (as a gentle rub with anything abrasive could ruin the optical quality) they fit a UV or skylight filter. These can then take the brunt of any damage and can easily be replaced. On the plus side your camera is always ready for action and the lens surface itself is always protected from the ingress of dust.

the lens

Conversely there are others who consider the use of any superfluous filter (not that UV or skylight filters are necessarily superfluous) is wrong. In truth is comes down to personal preference.

Whatever you decide it is important to ensure that your optical surfaces – whether lens or filter – remain clean at all times. Soft blower brushes are best for removing dust and pollution, and lint-free cotton cloths for fingerprints. Though it is not recommended by any lens manufacturer, a clean corner of a cotton shirt can be pressed into service when traditional cleansers are unavailable. As for damp and liquid cleaners exercise caution. If a lens is so soiled that only a liquid cleaner will suffice you may be better having the lens professionally cleaned; there is a risk when using fluids near lenses that some of the liquid can penetrate the gaps between the lens elements.

Camera driving

You won't be using your camera just to record video. You'll be reviewing scenes on location, playing the raw footage back in the studio (or your lounge) and exporting the same raw footage to your image editing application. Using the camcorder as a VCR can be taxing on all components of the tape system. Video heads have a finite lifetime after which the wear due to the tape rubbing against them will cause image degradation of new recordings and the replay of old. As replaying your recordings repeatedly will contribute to wear as much as recording it makes sense to limit the number of replays. Get the footage on to the computer as quickly as possible and, if you envisage a great number of requests prior to editing, copy the tape to VHS and save the originals until it is time to edit.

Summary

Getting to know your camera is essential for good moviemaking. Though many of your shots will be planned or will rely on the camera being set to 'auto', shots will present themselves that need rapid thinking and rapid shooting. Only with a complete knowledge of the camera and its controls will you be able to best record these.

Do spend some time getting to know what all the controls do – not all at once, but as you become increasingly comfortable with the basic controls.

And don't forget the manuals. Though this chapter has provided an overview it can be no more than that. Only the manuals give you the detail of your specific model.

13 basic video technique

In this chapter you will learn:
- about composition
- how to use different shot types
- about creating a shooting script and storyboard.

Though this book is principally concerned with digital video editing, some knowledge of basic video technique is essential if you are to record footage that is both appropriate to and of value to your video production. Over the next few chapters we will explore the real power of the digital tool chest that is our camcorder and how to use those tools to craft footage that will be the basis of our video production.

There are two essentials for creating great movies. One is getting raw footage that can ultimately be used to tell our story. We'll be looking at the process of shooting footage with a view to editing in the next chapter. But before that we need to understand and practise good film technique. Technique is a very important part of crafting good movies so we can only scrape the surface here. Though no guarantees can be made, an attention to the detail of these techniques will make your movie projects that bit better. Through this chapter we'll first examine shot types and framing scenes. Later we'll move on to the process of creating a script and how this can help us set up and capture the shots required to tell a story.

A sharp image

There is something of a conundrum in camcorder design. The cameras are clearly designed to be hand held and are expertly sculpted with that in mind. Yet read any book on technique – including in many cases those instructions and guides that accompany the camera itself – and you'll be strongly advised to bolt the camera to a tripod to get the best shots! How do we resolve this?

There is no doubt that a camera support of some kind helps to deliver steady shots that your audience will later appreciate. The hand friendly design of camcorders, coupled with image stabilization devices, means that it is also possible to get pretty steady shots when you hand hold. Decisions about whether you use a support or hand hold should be determined by the type of movie project you are undertaking.

When making a casual video of a family day out, hand holding will be quite sufficient (and the setting up of tripods or other supports will win you no favours). In fact hand holding is arguably better suited to the intimacy of such events.

A more formal production will usually demand steadier shots though some documentary-type presentations will also benefit from hand holding.

Of course there will be caveats in either case. For that family day out you may want to get everyone – including the cameraman – in the shot. Similarly those engaged in dramatic productions (the conventional candidate for steady shots) will quote the success of the *Blair Witch Project*, filmed with virtually no evidence of tripod use.

Standing still

The tripod is the conventional support for any camera. Virtually every model is incredibly stable, adjustable to most terrain and adjustable – within reasonable limits – to height. Refer back to Chapter 2 for some more comments about tripods.

Even if you do not want to carry a tripod there's no reason why your shots should be compromised. Almost any steady surface can be pressed into use either to rest the camera on or act as supplementary support. Drop a small beanbag into your gadget bag and you extend your options further. Beanbags provide maleable supports that can be used with impromptu supports to ensure the camera is level.

Understanding composition

As techniques go, more words have been written about composition than anything else. Picture composition is about placement of elements within a scene to best effect. This will relate to the relative positions of subjects in the frame and also how the different planes interact – foreground, background and subject plane.

There are plenty of rules expounding perfect or 'ideal' composition and those who make such rules often seem to spend all their time breaking them. In truth there are no hard and fast rules but there are compositions that seem to work better than others.

One of the most common, which applies also in still photography, is the Rule of Thirds. Newcomers seem to have an almost subconscious desire to place the subject of a scene bang in the centre of the frame. Where this subject is a person this usually means placing their head at the geometric centre. When you watch the resulting footage the result is a bit odd and very boring to watch. Using the rule of thirds to compose the scene will result in a far more effective frame.

Imagine the frame is divided into equal thirds both horizontally and vertically. Subjects (and other scene elements) contribute more powerfully to the composition if they are on these imaginary lines. For example, a person standing on one vertical line with their eye line at the point where a horizontal line bisects will have a very powerful screen presence. But this effect is not restricted to people. Placing your horizon line along the top third or bottom third line gives a far more pleasing result than placing it centrally or closer to the top or bottom.

Often the most potent compositions occur when the principal subject is at one intersection of the third lines and a foreground element (or, equally, a background one) is placed at the opposite as shown here.

Note too that some digital cameras feature an electronic grid that can be invoked to place a rule of thirds grid on the viewfinder or LCD screen. Of course, this grid is not recorded on the movie, but it can be a help in fine tuning your composition.

the rule of thirds

Shot sizes and types

There's no doubt that a video shot entirely from a single position is particularly dull. Consider that school play where the camera was propped up on a climbing frame for the whole performance. The patience of most good-natured viewers, looking forward to seeing their children's performance, will be sorely tested before scene two begins. Not only that, but when their child does appear they are likely to be so small on screen that the production will hardly stir memories. Your audience will watch patiently and then leave without further comment. Is that really the impression that you want to leave them with?

No, a polished production will require that you use shots from different angles and different positions. But for best effect these different positions must not be chosen haphazardly and any angles or positions adopted must be used with a purpose. Let's look at the mechanics of shots and how these different shot types can be used to build a movie sequence.

Distance-based shots

The fundamental shot types comprise a range where the difference is in the perceived camera-to-subject distance. These are perhaps more correctly defined in terms of the relative sizes of the subject and the surroundings. These shots are shown, comparatively, in colour plate 1.

The long shot (LS)

Often used to establish a location, the long shot (sometimes called a wide shot) uses the camera's lens set to a wide angle of view to take in the principal subject along with a significant amount of the surroundings. A figure would accommodate around two-thirds of the height of the screen and if they were engaged in an activity (such as playing football or even gardening) we would be able to see them in context. The extreme long shot (ELS) is the term given to the widest view that might comprise a wide sweeping landscape. ELSs tend to be used infrequently and need to be used with care (especially on home movies) as detail is very limited when the shot is viewed on a conventional television screen.

The medium shot (MS)

This identifies the subject within the landscape of the long shot. In doing so we begin to discover more about the subject (whether a person or an object) and are given some indications about the purpose or theme of the movie. This would be ideal for including a group of people together with sufficient detail for us to see their facial expressions.

The medium close-up (MCU)

This provides a view that is somewhat more than the head and shoulders of a close-up (below) wherein the subject is now the dominant element of the frame and emphasis is taken away from the background and surroundings. If our subject is, for example, two people engaged in conversation, this would be the ideal shot to accommodate both in a single frame.

The close-up (CU)

Now there is no mistaking the subject. Presuming the subject is a person, that person's head and shoulders are now filling the frame and we, as viewers, are able to concentrate on expression and intonation in their face. The big close-up (BCU) and extreme close-up (ECU) can add drama. In the case of the former the shot would include only the face of a subject, so that every line, wrinkle and expressive muscle movement is visible. The ECU like the ELS needs to be used with care. In this case the detail shown can lead to very powerful shots. For example, you might fill the frame with a subject's eyes to convey an expression of horror. Or, at a wedding you can stage a shot (as this is often impossible to do live) that features a ring being placed on the bride or groom's finger.

In Chapter 16 we'll be looking at how we can employ particular techniques such as jump cuts and cutting on the action to effect changes between types of shot – say from long shot to close-up or medium shot to long shot in a way that helps enhance the storyline and builds professionalism into your production.

Angle-based shots

Possibly described as more creatively motivated, angle-based shots use different camera angles to achieve particular effects. They comprise low and high angles along with some more contextual types.

High shot

Looking down on a subject tends to diminish his or her (or its) importance. This has the obvious effect of making the subject appear more vulnerable, weak or more humble. There is also a tendency for human subjects to appear more childlike, while pets appear docile. Because the effect is so striking such shots need to be used with care and generally only when such a specific look is required.

Low shot

The converse of the high shot, the low shot requires equal care in use as it imparts a sense of dominance and potency. Hence Low Shots can be used with great effect if you wish to show your subject as authoritative or commanding. It can also make your subject appear quite threatening.

low shots can give a sense of drama, or 'place' as these examples show

Note that the intermediate shot, wherein the camera is pretty well on the eye level of the subject, is often called a neutral shot. In keeping with the intermediate stance, these shots can evoke feelings of empathy and warmth towards the subject.

POV shots

The types of shot we've described above are all voyeur shots: they let the audience eavesdrop on activities and action. The POV shot – Point of View shot – lets the audience adopt the position of a character and see the world through his or her eyes.

You might use a POV shot in the following situation. In the first, establishing shot, you show a child watching television, lying on the floor. The following POV shot gives the view that the child has, taking in the television.

Over the shoulder shots

If using a POV shot in the case of the child watching television seems too dramatic, a more subtle way to visualize the child's perspective and view is to take an over the shoulder shot. Again the audience will share the subject's view of the world but the subject, in a sense, frames the shot.

Any of these shots can be taken at an appropriate distance from the subject, but in most cases medium shots through to close-ups represent the most effective distances.

Crane shots

Craning shots involve camera movement to draw attention to the subject of the shot. The mechanics of a crane is to begin with a foreground element usually taken from a very low position. The camera then rises to reveal more of the landscape beyond. In a wedding video the shot might begin with a close-up of the cake – or maybe a floral display – and is panned up to show an establishing shot of the wedding reception.

The Dutch tilt

Deliberately exaggerated perspective lies at the heart of the Dutch tilt, a shot used either for dramatic effect or to enhance certain characteristics of a scene. An often used example is to take a shot of a tall building from very close to the base looking almost directly up. There is strong convergence of the verticals and a very strong composition.

for large buildings, close up is often the only way of getting the whole subject in the frame

with a less steep angle the Dutch tilt also makes for a more interesting composition when used with discretion

Camera height

The message conveyed by your shot can be strongly affected by the height of the camera, as we alluded to in the case of a neutral shot. There is something very natural about using the camcorder at eye level and standing upright. We are used to viewing the world from our own eye level so why not record scenes from the same height? The problem is that shooting everything from this height can make for very boring movie footage. At waist level you place yourself at the head height of children and magically appear to enter their world. Go lower still and place the camera on the ground and you have another perspective altogether where everything and everyone assumes the role of giants.

With these alternate viewpoints there is nothing to stop you further enhancing the shot by adopting the angle of a low shot or, in the case of children playing, a low level over the shoulder shot.

Zooming

Your camera's zoom lens is a great compositional tool. You can use it to frame a subject precisely without moving your position. Okay, so that is being lazy! And the perspective may be better by moving the camera and retaining a wider-angle view, but that does not affect the zoom lens's power to bring distant objects closer.

Use of the zoom while filming is an effect that is usually frowned upon. It is generally regarded that the subjects of a scene should be the elements that move, not the camera. The zoom should be used only for framing. There are, however, situations where using the zoom while filming gives very powerful results. The slow zoom in to one face in a crowd is an often-used effect that, handled well, is not clichéd. Conversely a slow zoom out is a great way to show a subject relative to their surroundings.

Fast zooms make for very dramatic, attention grabbing scenes. But these are successful only if the zoom really is fast and focus is maintained. Competency in this effect will depend somewhat on the efficacy and control offered by the camera itself. There is a tendency for the fastest zoom speed to be a little pedestrian for this application and for the autofocus mechanism to hunt for best focus only once the zoom is complete. If you don't have a fast zoom a jump cut (p.215) might be an acceptable alternative.

So far as focusing is concerned, if there is any compromise, make it at the original focal length. Lock the focus at the zoomed-in point and accept a loss of critical sharpness when zoomed out – hopefully the impact of the zoom will avoid your audience noticing.

Modern digital cameras have, as we have noted, quite extensive zoom ratios that enable the zooming in, if required, to a subject that initially appears very small in the frame. Sadly, for all the technology, very few zoom lenses offer sufficient control for a carefully composed zoom action in a shot. Often only '+' and '-' zoom buttons (corresponding to zoom in and zoom out) are offered. If you are lucky these will be slightly pressure sensitive so that a firm press will deliver a faster zoom than a light one. But a subtle, steady zoom is often very difficult to achieve. A manual zoom handle, which permitted such action, is now confined only to the most expensive of cameras.

Do remember that the different focal lengths of a zoom lens can alter the perspective of a shot. You can show a subject at the same size – relative to the frame – with the lens at a wide angle or telephoto setting. In the former case you'll also include a substantial amount of background; with the telephoto setting the subject is more effectively isolated.

the wide angle shot   the telephoto shot

Choosing your backgrounds

The fact that your scenes will generally feature a subject of some kind dictates that this subject needs to be the focus of attention. Make it easy for your audience by placing that subject in an environment where the background (and, for that matter, the foreground) does not compete with the subject for attention. While a very plain background will often look unnatural (and might suggest that the shot has been specially staged) being observant and taking a few precautions will mean your scenes will be much more effective. If nothing else, it will save you time when it comes to the editing stage.

Getting the background right all the time is difficult, particularly if you are new to movie making. We all tend to get obsessed with our subject and getting the photography of them right; even the most experienced moviemaker occasionally overlooks the scenery over his or her shoulder.

Here are some suggestions for making the background less distracting:

- Use the zoom lens to fill the screen with the subject. This has the added bonus of reducing the depth of field in the scene (i.e. the amount of the scene in front or behind the subject that is in focus) so that the background will be somewhat blurred.
- Change the camera angle: a large nearby tree, for example, will be less distracting than similar, more distant ones further down the road.
- Move your subject closer to a backdrop (such as a wall, fence or foliage) or shoot from a slightly lower angle so that the sky provides the backdrop. This also removes foreground detail.

Creating a shooting script

Whether you propose to create that mini blockbuster, cover a social event or record a family day out you'll need to have some objectives and an overall vision. Ask yourself questions such as:

- What is the aim of this movie?
- Who is, or are, the intended audience?
- How much time do I propose to invest in it?
- What is the mood and tone?
- Does it require a script?

Some may be obvious to the point of absurdity but in asking them we help focus.

What is the aim of this movie?

This might seem obvious – we want to record something. That 'something' could be an event, a trip or holiday, or a documentary of some kind. But ask yourself whether the purpose – irrespective of the subject – is to entertain, enlighten or inform. Or is it to be a pure (and unemotive) record?

Who is, or are, the intended audience?

There is absolutely nothing wrong with producing a movie for your personal enjoyment but that movie director in you is probably going to want to share that enjoyment more widely. Knowing and understanding any audience is very important to determining the content. If your video may be shown widely you'll want to avoid personal or potentially embarrassing elements. More select audiences may have different needs and expectations. Imagine you have recorded your family's visit to a preserved railway. If you are asked to show the movie to some train enthusiasts they are unlikely to be enamoured by shots of the family enjoying the ride and having a picnic afterwards. Conversely the children's grandparents will be unimpressed by detailed views of 2-4-2 tank engines.

Note, as we did earlier, that if the movie is being produced for the specific application of Web delivery there are certain rules that need to be followed to best exploit the limitations of this medium.

How much time do I propose to invest in it?

When we talk about investing time in the movie, it raises some important issues and some subsidiary questions. Clearly when we have been asked – or even commissioned – to produce a wedding video we must be very focused on the project and totally committed to delivering a first-rate production. Conversely, if we are recording a family day out we may not want the mechanics of movie making to interfere with our and our family's enjoyment of the day. It is to be expected that parts of a wedding might be re-shot specifically for the camera, but re-shooting a roller coaster ride at a theme park may be out of the question (and try the patience of our surrogate actors).

The question of time investments will also apply the post-production phase. A largely impromptu movie of our day out may not demand much in terms of post-production editing. It may be sufficient merely to remove redundant footage. Our social commission, however, may need a substantial amount of work to tell a good story and to best present the footage gathered at the event.

What is the mood and tone?

It is important to define the tone of your movie early on. Are you aiming for a reportage type look where the camera is obviously hand held or something more formal? Do you want the tone light and frivolous or somewhat darker? Making such decisions will impact on how you structure and frame your shots.

Does it require a script?

It's wrong to assume that because your movie is not obviously a drama it will not require a script. A shooting script, detailing (or at least providing an overview) of the shots required, is pretty much essential if your editing is to be successful. Miss a scene and you'll be hard pressed to make good the omission at the editing stage. The wedding video is an obvious example of a movie that will require a shooting script to ensure that all elements are recorded. Fortunately weddings (and most other social events) are so rigorously proscribed that a script can be created that applies to any future events you may record. Even if you are planning to record something informal – such as our family day out – a shooting script will be useful, but can be equally informal. In some of these cases you can gather the footage first and write the script after; where there is not a structured story that needs telling it is quite feasible to review your footage and construct the movie around the available resources.

Scripting and storyboarding

If you have determined your movie requires a script then you'll need to spend some time formulating one. If you have never done so before this can seem a little daunting. Where do you begin? How much detail do you need? Difficult questions to answer, and questions that will vary according to the subject of the movie. Let us consider the wedding video. Denominational issues apart, such events cover a sequence that is probably well known to all those who attend. Drawing up a shooting script for a wedding will involve little more than listing the sequence of events. Here's a typical one:

Wedding service
- early day preparations, bride and/or groom
- location shots of venue (church or otherwise)
- bridesmaids and pages preparing and arriving at venue
- guests arriving (parents of couple especially)
- congregation chatting prior to service
- groom and best man waiting
- entry of the bride
- service (exchange of vows)
- signing of the register
- married couple leaving.

The reception
- guests arriving and being greeted by couple
- dinner scenes (can also be used as cutaways)
- speeches
- dancing and conversation.

Clearly this is something of an overview, rather than a scene-by-scene description of events. The number of scenes showing guests arriving will depend on the number of guests, for example, while coverage of the service itself may depend upon any regulations in force at the venue. In all cases such as this it's essential that you make yourself aware of any restrictions. Some venues prohibit the use of cameras of any sort, others have restrictions during parts of ceremonies. Others may limit access to the photographer. It is important not only to respect any such restrictions but to appreciate the need for them and modify your script to account for them.

Don't – either – let a list like this restrict you. Treat it as a list of those episodes that need to be filmed; other, impromptu scenes that make the day memorable should also be recorded. We can always discard them if they prove inappropriate later. The photographer arranging family members, guests in hats battling against strong winds and mischievous toddlers can make the movie more enjoyable and more personal.

If your production is to be more dramatic (in the theatrical sense) then a shooting script is pretty much essential. Furthermore, it is usually augmented by a storyboard. You've probably seen these in those 'Making of . . .' documentaries that explain (often in tedious detail) all the stages of a major movie's production. Drawn using cartoon-like characters, storyboards let those involved in the movie production decide how each scene should look. Not only do they show who (or what) should be in each scene, they also illustrate the type of shot required and how each shot fits into the sequence. Matters such as continuity are easily assessed along with the need for any special additional shots.

There is often the supposition that a storyboard is something fatuous and superfluous. Once you have produced your first dramatic movie you'll realize the importance of one, particularly when it comes to the editing stage. Don't worry if your drawing skills leave a little to be desired; the storyboard is for your personal use. As long as you can understand the meaning that will be ample.

Summary

Remember: good technique is based on good practice and experience yet all of us occasionally suffer sloppy technique. Think before you shoot and think especially of how you want to the finished film to appear.

14

light and lighting

In this chapter you will learn:
- about the different types of lighting
- how cameras respond in low light conditions
- how to use auxiliary lighting.

The light that illuminates our video footage is something we either take for granted or, due to our location, have to take for granted. Light is all around us and, within reasonable limits, digital video cameras are able to adapt to the available light (usually termed the ambient light) and set the exposure accordingly. Though we do generally tend only to acknowledge the presence of sufficient illumination before shooting, a little more understanding about the way lighting works and how to exploit it will help further enhance our movie productions.

It is important to recognize that although lighting is essential to video photography – as it is to photography in general – good lighting and thoughtful lighting will help make the crucial difference between a memorable movie and a lacklustre one.

Contre-jour

Often given the more descriptive term 'backlighting' contre-jour means having the principal light source behind the subject. It does not necessarily mean the light is immediately behind the subject (and consequently throwing it into silhouette) but generally behind the subject such that the subject's back is the most strongly illuminated side. Taken from the French and meaning 'against the light' contre-jour lighting can either be very dramatic or render scenes unwatchable. In the case of camcorders, which invariably have automatic exposure control, it is the latter. The camera will compensate for the strong lighting and close down the aperture, rendering your subject very dark. Even if your camera has advanced metering control this type of lighting will generally fool it and you will find that the surroundings, rather than the subject, are determining exposure.

contre-jour lighing can be dramatic but usually compromises the subject

The simple solution is to avoid backlighting wherever possible; try to configure the angle between the light source, the subject and the camera such that it is never more than 90 degrees. When this is not practical try one of the following:

- Select backlight compensation. Though not all cameras feature this, selecting backlight compensation will increase the aperture to allow in more light (usually by a factor of two to four times) preventing the subject being over-darkened. This does not affect the difference in illumination between the subject and the background so it is near certain that the background will become substantially over exposed.

- Use a video light. A supplementary video light attached to the camera (or supported on a tripod nearby) will provide additional lighting to the subject and lessen the contrast between it and the background. In this case the background stands less of a chance of becoming overexposed. This technique is very similar to using fill-in flash in conventional photography.

- Use a reflector. Because in contre-jour the light will probably also be striking the photographer, you can use a reflector to reflect the light source back at the subject, with a similar effect to using a video light. Such reflectors are often purpose made. The models from Lastolite are particularly effective in that they come in different colours and fold away when not required. Choose silver for a neutral reflection, gold for a very warm and intermediate for a warm effect that is particularly flattering for skin tones. In the absence of a custom device you can always improvise, pressing a white tablecloth into service, for example.

It is possible to make corrections to your footage whilst editing. You could, for example, alter the brightness and contrast controls to remove as much of the contre-jour shading as possible, but getting the footage right in the first place is usually a more effective solution.

Direct *vs.* indirect lighting

Bright sunlight can be terrific. It provides plenty of light, can deliver really vibrant colours and gives excellent contrast and depth to your shots. But, for most of the day, the same bright sunlight can be problematic, casting deep shadows that, when on subjects' faces, are deeply unflattering. When wrinkles and extra chins are emphasized your subjects will not be too enamoured. Furthermore, even if those subjects are facing away from the light, the very high ambient lighting levels are likely to cause them to squint or grimace.

The solution is to use indirect lighting wherever possible. Again, this is often easier said than done, but indirect illumination will soften shadows and create a more even illumination. Indirect illumination doesn't necessarily mean shade or shadow areas, but those regions of the scene principally illuminated by light reflected from walls, buildings and even deliberately set reflectors. The light levels will not be that much less than in full sunlight (so far as the camera is concerned) but the results will be far superior. You'll be able to match a richness of colour with natural pose and posture.

Time of day and colour temperature

Direct lighting is at its most harsh during the two hours either side of midday. This is the time when (in the summer months at least) the sun is high in the sky and subject shadows are the most profound. Conversely, closer to sunrise and sunset the light is somewhat softer. There is another change that takes place. Around midday the light is white (or neutral) and colours are at their most authentic. As we examine the light at the extremes of the day the colour balance moves towards the warmer colours – yellow, orange and red. This gives an emotional feeling of warmth to your scenes that – depending, of course, on the subject matter – can also appear more romantic. The penalty is that the change in colour balance will render some colours (particularly blues and greens) somewhat muddier than they would have appeared at midday. You will also tend to lose detail in the shot. While this may not be important for human subjects (where the warmth of the light appears more flattering) it might compromise landscapes, where the midday light might be more appropriate.

Though many people find it a little abstract, a good way of comparing the colour balance of light sources is to use colour temperature. Colour temperatures are actually determined by measuring the colour and quality of light radiating from a 'perfect radiator' at different temperatures. From this we can correlate different kinds of lighting and the lighting found at different times of the day with a colour temperature value. The values for some typical sources are shown in Table 7. The temperature is indicated according to the Kelvin scale (K) which is almost exactly equivalent to the Centigrade temperature + 273 degrees.

Table 7

Source	Colour temperature (K)
Blue sky (no clouds)	18,000
Sunlight sky, moderate haze	10,000
Shade and shadows, summer	8,000
Continuous overcast sky	7,000
Light overcast Sky	6,500
Average daylight	6,400
Mean noonday light	5,400
Early morning/evening sun	4,500
Post-dawn/pre-sunset	3,700
Standard photoflood tungsten light	3,400
Halogen video lamp	3,300
100w GLS lightbulb	2,750
Sunrise/sunset	2,000
Candle	1,500

To summarize the table cold, blue colours tend to have a very high colour temperature while warm, red colours have a low colour temperature. If this seems slightly twisted logic imagine the case of coals in a fire. When they are burning at their coolest they are red. As the temperature rises they become orange and then yellow. If it was possible to heat them even higher we would see the colours move increasingly towards the cooler blue.

In professional photography and cinematography the colour temperature can be very important. In such cases colour temperature meters are used to measure the colour temperature of a scene (or part of the scene) very accurately. It is very unlikely that we will need such colour accuracy on our productions. In any case the darkroom effects in the post-production editing stage include filters to alter the colour balance.

White balance

When we discussed features of digital camcorders we made mention of the white balance feature. This, as you might recall, adjusted the recording of a scene so that lighting values were 'averaged' to a neutral white. This, for practical purposes, compensates for changes in colour temperature in most circumstances. But this feature is often so effective that it can neutralize the very colour casts – such as those at sunrise and sunset – that you are trying to record. Hence most white balance controls can be switched from auto to a range of presets, designed for specific lighting situations. A typical range of presets will include:

- auto: fully automatic calibration
- sunlight: balanced for mean sunlight (use this setting to preserve light quality at the extremes of the day)
- broken cloud: balanced to the mixed lighting of a sunny day with some cloud cover
- overcast: balanced for overcast skies
- tungsten: compensates for the reddish amber cast produced by standard household GLS tungsten bulbs
- fluorescent: compensates for the specific colour properties of fluorescent lightning. This can produce warm, magenta or even green colour casts and hence many cameras feature three fluorescent presets, one for each cast. Note that energy saving bulbs (often denoted as SL or PL) are derivatives of fluorescent technology.

Keeping the camera set to auto will leave you prepared for most eventualities. It is also the best setting if you have a mix of lighting types. Though the auto setting will largely compensate for extremes (such as removing the tungsten lighting casts), switching to a dedicated preset can sometimes be more effective.

Amount of light

Our eyes are so adept at adjusting to different lighting levels that it is difficult to appreciate how significant the changes in light level can be, in absolute terms. With a few conditions that we will address in a moment camcorders are equally adept. The measurement of light intensity is the Lux and in Table 8 the Lux levels for different lighting situations are listed.

Table 8

Scene type	Lux
Sunlit beach or snowfield	100,000
Sunlit scene in summer	50,000
Sunlit scene in winter	15,000
Overcast sky	5,000
Subjects lit at sunrise/sunset	500
Brightly lit room	250
Urban street lighting	50
Dusk/candlelit scene	5–10

'Sunlight' presumes clear sky with no high altitude clouds.

It has become increasingly important to camera manufacturers to quote the lowest lux level at which a camera will successfully record an image. This is not necessarily for practical reasons but often marketing ones – it helps give certain models a perceived edge when comparisons are made with models from other manufacturers.

whether lighting is dim or bright, your camcorder is adept at recording the scene

Low light performance

Some camcorders are even able to work in total darkness; using image-intensifying technology they can amplify the tiny amount of background illumination to create an acceptable image. Though this has been ascribed a gimmick it does have some genuine uses, even if the results give a somewhat unworldly look to any human or animal subjects recorded.

In practice, working at very low light levels is not the best option. Here are some reasons not to shoot at low light levels, or not to use low light conditions more than is absolutely necessary.

- Video noise. The electronics of the camera and the CCD chip itself produce a certain amount of electronic noise that is randomly distributed across the picture. Though this is normally minor when compared with the signal (that is, the images) being recorded, at low signal levels (dark scenes) the noise is more significant. It becomes a more significant contributor to the overall image resulting in the picture becoming fuzzier and more uncomfortable to watch.
- Dynamic range. Dynamic range is a measure of the difference between the darkest and lightest part of the image. The greatest range occurs between black shadows and white highlights. At low light levels the dynamic range is very compressed, limiting the range of brightness levels (and, consequentially, colours) that we normally expect in an image. The viewers are presented with a somewhat muddy scene that, combined with video noise, is increasingly less watchable as the light levels diminish.
- Picture information. At low levels (largely as a result of video noise and dynamic range) there is less picture information recorded. Hence when we reach the post-production phase we are limited in how much remedial action we can take to enhance an image. Scenes taken in bright sunlight can be manipulated (using filters to alter the overall brightness and contrast, for example) but those taken in darker situations can rarely be improved.

If you are aiming to record, say, a candlelit scene then film it using supplementary lighting such as carefully directed room lighting or even exterior lighting from an overcast sky. Your footage may not be as intimate as you intended but you will have better dynamic range, lower noise levels (as a proportion of the total signal) and better opportunities to create the required ambience in post production.

Auxiliary lighting

Cine photographers were handicapped to a certain extent by having film stock that was somewhat limited in sensitivity and allowed little latitude in exposure. Hence indoor photography by available or ambient lighting was rarely successful. Although in the latter years cine photography was bolstered by faster (i.e. more sensitive) films, most photographers had to resort to powerful auxiliary lights to film interiors successfully. These very powerful lights (with outputs of up to 1000 watts) would provide the necessary lighting but often at the expense of dazzling the subjects.

More modest auxiliary lights are available for camcorder use, featuring both mains and battery power. The higher sensitivity of the video camera means that lighting need not be so powerful as the cine equivalent and these lights tend to find use where it is necessary to prevent the video noise that might otherwise result. Designed to be camera mounted, care has to be taken to avoid getting flat results and unusual shadows; it is often more successful to use them in bounce mode (where the light is directed at and reflects from the ceiling) or to mount the unit on a separate (fixed) tripod.

direct lighting is harsher (though more powerful) than bounce lighting (right)

15
recording sound

In this chapter you will learn:
- about sound and sound levels
- which microphone is the best to use
- how to record and use ambient sound.

Sound, as we suggested earlier, should not be considered secondary to the visual elements. For a coherent video production we need to have sounds and images that together help produce experiences that are entirely complementary. True, we can look at images (photographs or even old silent movies) without sound as we can enjoy sound without any accompanying visuals but when a movie is coupled with an appropriate soundtrack it becomes much more immersive for the viewer. Here we'll look at the sound recording capabilities our camcorders feature and consider at the options available if we wish to extend those capabilities. We'll also take a look at the importance of ambient sound.

Time was when sound was recorded quite separately from the images (then film, rather than video) and were we writing this book in those days much of the content of this chapter would be concerned with ensuring sound and vision remained in synchronization.

Now we have no such worries; digital camcorders not only record pretty good sound but this sound is perfectly synchronized to the picture. All the user need do is turn on the camera and press record. But like so much of the video production process we can make this good sound even better. Partly through technique and partly using hardware we'll examine the ways in which we can record – at the time of filming – sound that will positively enhance your movie. Let's begin by getting an appreciation of two of the basic characteristics of sound, levels and quality.

Sound levels

As with the light levels, the sounds we wish to record can comprise a very wide range from the softest whisper to the roar of a jet taking off overhead. We use the decibel scale for measuring sound levels where, using a logarithmic scale, an increase of three decibels is equivalent to a doubling in the sound pressure.

Table 9

Sound	Decibels (dB)
Large jet aircraft at take off	125
Tube train interior	94
Motorway traffic (from overbridge)	84
Car interior	70
Conversation	60
Whispers	20
'silence'	9

Because the intensity of sound varies with our distance from it, Table 9 gives only an indication of the sound levels; actual levels will vary according to distance from source.

When you record sound with your camcorder, unless you have a professional or semi-pro model, you'll find that recording levels are set automatically. This is both a blessing and a curse.

It is a blessing because, whether your source is that jet taking off or a whisper, you can be assured that the recording level will always be optimum. The curse comes when you want a particularly loud or quiet sound recorded. You will find that the delicate nuances (or floor-shaking depth) are somewhat reduced. You will also find that (to some degree) the recording is clipped or amplified respectively. In the same way that automatic audio recording equipment restricts (or 'limits') sound levels, so those recorded on tape can be compromised.

Sound quality

Being one of the first media to offer digital technology the CD audio disc has set the benchmark in audio quality. Despite the protestations of audiophiles who are possibly alone in being able to discern the shortcomings, CD audio has defined the standard to which other audio media – such as the sound component of DVD and digital television – must aspire.

Similarly this benchmark has been one of the criteria used to differentiate digital video cameras from analogue models. Though it is true that the digital video format is capable of recording sound of a comparable quality, the actual sound recorded may not achieve such heights. Various compromises dictated by price and size may limit the quality you can record, particularly if you are limited to the onboard built-in microphones.

Microphones

What we lose in absolute quality when using the built-in microphone we gain in practicality. Let's take a look at its strengths and weaknesses; we can then examine whether it will be sufficient for the needs of your movie productions.

- Convenience. There is an argument that there is no excuse for ever forgetting any piece of kit. But, be honest, we all do it sometime. With a built-in microphone even the most forgetful of us has no excuse for being caught dumb. And should you have assessed that an auxiliary microphone is in order then you've a back-up (or reserve).

- Omnidirectionality. The built-in microphone is necessarily a jack of all trades and will pretty successfully record all sounds that it is exposed to. Like all compromises it is only 'good' at recording various sounds (from ambient sound though to interviews) it does not excel at any. But sometimes good is not good enough. Directionality is often important in recording sound, either because we only want to record the sound immediately in front or (as it can be an important contributor to sound ambience) we need to record the acoustics to either side also.

- Camera whirr. Because the built-in microphone is so successful at recording all incoming sounds it is also adept at recording the motor sounds from the camcorder itself. Fortunately most models are very quiet in operation and so this element is not as significant as it might be, but it can still prove a distraction during quiet spells.

- Wind noise. Similarly there is a propensity to recording wind noise. External microphones can be fitted with a wind baffle (the little furry gloves that sometimes creep into shot on location TV broadcasts) but not so built-in ones. To be effective they would be so large as to interfere with the lens. You can limit wind noise by careful shielding but the emphasis has be on careful. Poor shielding can create a poor sound image.

- Distance. The sound volume reduces with distance from the camera. This roughly follows the inverse square law: a sound source at a certain distance from the camera will be four times louder than the same source at twice the difference. Most built-in microphones are designed to work best with sound sources no more than 10 metres from the camera. Note too that when you use the zoom lens to focus in on an element of your scene the microphone does not do likewise. When the movie is being viewed this incongruity may prove troublesome for viewers. Think of the microphone as a fixed lens. As a fixed lens always provides the same angle of video so the built-in microphone provides a similarly fixed sound stage.

The external microphone

The solution to the built-in microphone's shortcomings is, somewhat obviously, an external microphone. As befits a specialist device there is no single solution to all sound recording situations, but rather a range of add ons, each of which is optimized to a particular sound source or recording situation. In some cases it is not possible to use an external microphone (there is simply no means of connecting one) but given that an increasing number of models feature an appropriate input, let's take a look at the options on offer.

That connection, by the way, is often a simple jack plug but on more advanced models (of microphone and camera) can comprise a multi-channel accessory shoe connection enabling the microphone's amplifiers to be powered by the camera and twin channel (stereo) sound recorded to tape.

Microphone types

Cardioid

Often sold as the 'standard' external microphone the cardioid features a sensitivity across a 200 degree arc in front of the camera. Its name is derived from the heart-shaped map of the microphone's sensitivity through a 360 degree arc. Though a good all-rounder it is particularly good at recording conversation at a distance up to four metres.

Supercardioid and hypercardioid

With 120 degree and 90 degree sensitivity these have similar characteristics to the cardioid but a greater sensitivity to the area in front of the camera. Hence they are effective at recording more distant conversation taking place in the camera's angle of view but have lower sensitivity to the sound on either side.

Zoom

This is a microphone that can be switched between cardioid and supercardioid to allow the sound recording to be more focused on the central area in front of the microphone. Some models offer improved zooming that is close to that of a hypercardioid. Note that some manufacturers market hypercardioid microphones as 'zoom' models on the pretext that they are designed to be used with zoom lenses.

Narration microphone

Made famous by news reporters, the narration microphone is omnidirectional – sensitive to sound from all directions – but is particularly well suited to the recording of speech. They tend to be used close to the mouth (which is why you see them being thrust into the faces of celebrities and politicians) to get the best balance between commentary and ambient sound. These models are also used in post-production (and can be used in video editing applications) to record commentaries.

Tie-clip microphone

A small microphone designed to be attached discretely (not surprisingly) to a speaker's tie or shirt. Again they tend to be omnidirectional and, for good recording levels, require that the speaker does not vary the position of his or her mouth in relation to the microphone too much.

Radio microphones

Most of the models of microphone are available as radio microphones, which avoid the problem of running (and concealing) a microphone cable from the microphone to the camera. They tend to be somewhat more expensive and can be prone to interference (both from general electrical noise and other environmental sources).

Ambient sound

Ambient sound can be crucial in conveying the atmosphere of a location. Be it traffic in the distance or the general 'buzz' of the city, without it your production will sound very flat.

Recording ambient sound for continuity

Certain ambient sounds – the sea breaking on the shore or children's howls on a fairground ride – are easy to record and will be perfectly synchronized with the event. Other sounds are no less important but can be problematic to record. Background music is a particular case in point. Such music can be important in conveying the mood of a party, say, or the ambience at a venue. But if we record scenes at the party or venue there are going to be discontinuities at scene breaks. If you are very lucky and the music is not too prominent you may get away with the breaks but in most cases you will not be so fortunate.

You've two options. The first, which is the easiest, is to record continuously. Get the shots you want, but rather than switching off the camera between this shot and the next, keep it running. It doesn't matter what you record in these intervals – you could even cover the lens to make it clear when editing what shots you did not want to keep.

When you have gathered all the required shots and the music has finished, record some cutaways (p.211). You can use these in the editing stage to replace only the video track for the 'in between' scenes, letting the soundtrack remain unbroken (the method of breaking a clip into audio and video tracks for this purpose is discussed on p.123). You have the benefit in this case of any conversations that may take place being in full synchronization.

The more complex method is to record the music separately and combine this with the appropriate video footage at the editing stage. This becomes particularly difficult if you need to synchronize sound with video, but for general scenes it can work well.

Of course there is another option – that is to record the appropriate music (from a CD or other source) and combine it with the video track later. This can work well if the music is at very low volume on the original soundtrack and other sounds (conversation etc.) are much more prominent. And if there is no specific dialogue you can always add another soundtrack channel with general conversation from an effects CD or some other recording that you might have in your archive. If you can control the event (which is usually easier at a small party than a concert venue) you can exploit short breaks in the music to record your footage. Adding your own music later then becomes much simpler.

Collecting ambient sounds

It is useful whenever on location to gather some ambient sounds. Again this can be done with the camcorder and recording no visual material. We can then use this sound to replace existing ambient sounds if something untoward has intruded. A plane flying overhead or an announcement over a public address system can all contrive to spoil your soundtrack. A bit of stock audio footage provides an easy solution.

16

shooting to edit

In this chapter you will learn
- how to shoot your movie
- about implementing specific techniques
- the interplay between different shots.

Shooting video for digital editing

Many eminently watchable movies result from the editing of video recordings made very casually and often with no script in mind. The power (and ease of use) of digital video makes this possible. We've seen that following a shooting script (even if it is a very 'loose' one, held in our heads) can make our production even better, ensuring we have no holes that will be impossible to fill. We can go further now and introduce some unscripted additional scenes that can be used to improve continuity further.

There are certain shots that you will find indispensable when you edit footage. These are crucial to creating a movie that flows well and has proper continuity. They are not shots that you might take as a matter of course having never edited a video before; their necessity is often borne from experience. As your movie-making prowess increases you'll note their importance and spend time collecting appropriate shots – even if many end up on the digital equivalent of the cutting room floor.

Build these shots into your shooting script and your editing will be simpler and the results much more professional:

- cutaways
- insert shots
- pickups
- establishing shots
- entrances and exits.

Cutaways

Cutaways are a powerful tool in achieving continuity in your productions. They enable a shot that would otherwise be overlong to be trimmed to a convenient length (by removing intermediate footage) without the cuts being obvious to the viewer. You will see cutaways used extensively in interview situations. Where the interviewee is giving a series of answers to questions posed a cutaway will be used to enable irrelevent questions or answers to be removed. At the cut point the visuals will change from a close-up of the interviewee to the interviewer nodding or, perhaps, a close-up of the interviewee's hands. Often these are called reaction shots, as it shows some reaction on the part of those involved.

Other cutaways use environmental shots to link parts of a conversation. Views of day-to-day life in a village could be used as cutaways in a video where a local resident talks about village life and we need to discard superfluous comment. Below are two typical shots that would be used as cutaways during an interview. The clasped hands (of the interviewee) are ideal as they can convey (through hand movements) the mood of the person. The shots of ornaments and room details give more of an insight to the person and their way of life.

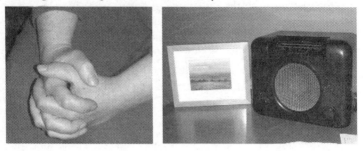

Insert shots

Like cutaways (of which Insert Shots are often described as specialized form) these provide visual continuity in a sequence. Unlike cutaways (where the implication is that the timeline is continuing throughout) insert shots are most often used to imply the passage of time.

Here are a couple of examples.

- The meeting: In the first shot a man is walking towards the door of a building. He looks at his watch (which shows 1 o'clock). An insert shot of a clock on the building shows 2 o'clock. The next scene shows the man walking out. The clear implication is that an hour has passed even though only minutes have passed in the filming log.
- School Christmas play: The video begins with the early rehearsals. Then an insert shot shows the doors of an advent calendar being opened up to that of the performance day. The next shot shows the main performance about to begin.

Pickups

Another specialized form of cutaway, the pickup is usually filmed after an event or sequence of shots (like some cutaways) to help join two parts of a sequence that, for some reason, have become separated. Taking the example of our interview, perhaps the interviewee has become very emotional and would like to take a break. Or, unforgivably, you as cameraman have run out of tape. A pickup scene might include a shot of the interviewer asking the question posed to the interviewee following the break and might include an acknowledgement of the answer to the previous question.

Establishing shots

Earlier we discussed the creation and use of titles. We noted how it was possible to imply surroundings or a location without the need for formal titles at all, letting the visuals do all the work. The shots that establish the location of the following scenes are known technically as establishing shots. They can be used to introduce the whole movie or, when the locations change, to introduce the new location. If the establishing shots you have taken prove not to establish the location with sufficient unambiguity they can always be recycled as the background for a more conventional title shot.

Note that you are generally establishing the location – the city you are visiting or the church in which a wedding is about to take place – so they should not feature any of the action relating to the visit or wedding. Hence you may need to record establishing shots before (or even after) the event.

entrance signage has been used as an establishing shot for this day out the second shot, a long shot, gives more information on the location prior to moving on to some more personal shots

Entrances and exits

Sometimes called clean entries, these are the most subtle of shots and unlike the previous examples, need to be written into the shooting script.

There are some forms of continuity error that you become aware of only after watching your movie several times. Your audience, however, is probably aware of it from the first showing. These are entrances and exits. Where your movie features characters (whether in a fictional or reportage presentation) it is important that they are seen – at some point – arriving at a location and, where appropriate, leaving.

Poor entries and exits are often seen on wedding movies. The bride arrives at the church and gets out of the car, cart or carriage. Her train and veil are adjusted and she prepares to walk to the church. In the next scene she is walking towards the entrance of the church. It seems quite obvious when you are both cameraman and director what is happening, but the audience will see a sudden 'jump'. This is the ideal place to interject an entrance scene taken from just inside the church gate. The bride comes through the gate and crosses the frame. Suddenly the geometry and continuity make sense to everyone. It is clear where the bride is coming from and where she is heading.

Keeping the line

There is one deceit practised extensively in moviemaking that, as a testament to its effectiveness, goes somewhat unnoticed. This is known as keeping the line. This technique is concerned with the geometry of the screen and our perceived geometry when viewing.

The head-on shot

Imagine a scene where two people, a man to the left and a woman to the right, are talking to each other and approaching the camera. They pass either side of the camera and in the next scene we see them walking away from the camera, continuing their conversation. It is only on closer – or perhaps repeat – inspection we notice something odd about the second scene. The man is still to the left! Had the scene shown the true geometry of this view from behind it should have been the woman to the left. We do this to prevent the viewers 'doing a double take' and being momentarily confused to the point where their attention is drawn away from the action.

The conversation

Now imagine our man and woman have sat down. We variously record scenes featuring the man (this time sitting to the left) and the woman (right) either individually or together. If we were – just to introduce some variety into the shots – to move around to the back so that the man is on the right, talking to the woman on the right we would have 'crossed the line' again. Our audience would immediately assume the two characters have been transposed and suffer momentary confusion again. Though they would soon reconcile the scenes it would be unsettling.

In both cases it is important that this imaginary (and, in a sense, fallacious) line is followed. Rather than shots from very different angles (in the case of 'The conversation') use cutaways instead.

Changing the shot

We established in Chapter 13 a range of shot types – from the extra long shot through to the extreme close-up – that perform different roles in presenting scenes to our viewers. What we have not done yet is look at how we change, creatively, from one to another. Let's take a look at two techniques – the jump cut and cutting on the action – that are useful here.

The jump cut

A jump cut uses a deliberate and abrupt change in shot between two scenes. This can be between any two shot types but the distinguishing feature is that the camera angle does not change. Where the first shot is a long shot and the second a close-up, the viewers are immediately drawn into the heart of the action; where the first is a medium shot and the second a long shot (or even an extreme long shot), a small feature or person is suddenly shown in the context of their surroundings.

Because of the nature of this type of transition it is often difficult (if not impossible) to achieve when recording live action. It needs to be staged with the subject or subjects remaining motionless when the second shot is configured. Any motion meantime will look patently obvious in the final production and a very visible continuity error appears.

Cutting on the action

This is another technique that needs to be staged as success depends on no changes in the action between the two scenes. Unlike the jump cut, this time we do not have to be so precious about the camera angles but do need to ensure continuity. Typical shots involving cutting on the action might comprise an initial scene of someone about to throw a ball. Just prior to the throw taking place we select a wider view – a medium shot for example – showing both the thrower and a second person to whom the ball is being thrown.

17
movie projects detailed

In this chapter you will learn:
- how to video a wedding
- how to video a child's birthday
- the best way to record other events.

The digital video techniques we have discussed so far are ideal for a number of projects that not only allow you to show off your creative skills but also give your friends, family and colleagues the chance to enjoy the fruits of your labours too. Here's a guide to some of the more popular, taking in some of the peripheral issues that go to making a production successful in technical and practical terms.

The wedding

Back in Chapter 13 we looked at scripting using a wedding movie as an example. Let's look now in a little more detail at the creation of such a video. Weddings probably represent the most videoed of occasions and if you have been commissioned to film one – or if you have commissioned yourself to make one – there will be plenty of others setting standards by which yours will be judged. Weddings are fantastic events for the movie maker but with all the emotion and sentiment of the day they can also be quite onerous.

If ever there was a case of doing it by the book the wedding video would be it. The nature of the event is such that every step has been planned to the proverbial nth degree and features stage management to a degree any theatrical performance would be proud of.

Preparations and the service
- early day preparations, bride and/or groom
- location shots of venue (church or otherwise)
- bridesmaids and pages preparing and arriving at venue
- guests arriving (parents of couple especially)
- congregation chatting prior to service
- groom and best man waiting
- entry of the bride
- service (exchange of vows)
- signing of the register
- married couple leaving
- confetti throwing
- throwing the corsage

The reception
- guests arriving and being greeted by couple
- dinner scenes (can also be used as cutaways)

- speeches
- dances and conversation
- the couple's departure

Useful cutaways and title shots
- church/location interiors
- the wedding invitation
- ceremonial cars parked
- reception table decorations and place name cards
- the wedding cake

Permissions

As we mentioned earlier some venues may require permission to film at certain locations or at certain times. In many cases there may be restrictions imposed. Rather than risk offence, it is a good idea to contact a representative of the venue well in advance to see what rules – if any – apply. In many cases regular venues, such as churches and registry offices, will provide the bride and groom with specific information that will include details of photography. If you are prevented in any way, accept the limitation and devise a work around. Don't be surprised either if you see the official photographer taking still photos in situations where you have been banned – there are often different rules for still and video photography.

Understanding needs

Discussions should also extend to the couple themselves. Even if you are recording a wedding as a favour to friends (or perhaps have been asked to do it by the family of the couple) it is important that you discuss the couple's desires beforehand. The video will be a record of their day, and it would be wrong to put your particular slant on it or produce it in a style that may not be to the couple's liking. As part of this discussion establish how intrusive the video can be. Many people still find video very intrusive and the presence of a video camera – no matter how discreet – stirs feelings that range from self-consciousness through to disapproval. Let this be a two-way discussion. If the couple are concerned about, say, the videoing of the service, demonstrate your video camera and how unobtrusive it can be. For example, you may like to demonstrate how you can place the camera on a beanbag in a window reveal overlooking the couple and the celebrant and operate it remotely. Such discretion can often win over those who might otherwise be resistant and provide very good footage.

Contingency

If you are limited in what you can film during the service don't despair. When you compile your movie, emphasize the preparations and the reception. Alternatively, keep the camera running through the vows with the intention of recording the sound of the event. You can then add visuals, such as still shots of the couple, later.

Inclusion and impartiality

Discuss, too, those people who should be given special prominence in the video. Establish a list of all those who will be attending and who to give this special prominence and attention to and – as is usually the case – who not to. And if you are not familiar with your cast – the families and friends – make sure there is someone with whom you can liaise to ensure all the guests are correctly identified.

Once you have identified – and recorded – everyone (usually as they arrive at the location) you'll have to take care that subsequently you are even handed about showing the guests, taking care not to favour one group (or one family) over another. There may be a terrific tenor who sounds and looks impressive throughout the singing but constant filming of him is likely to be frowned upon by those who feel upstaged. Look out, too, for that camera-shy person that could so easily be overlooked. Families are often particularly aware of such members and are delighted if you manage to include them.

It is difficult to know how much, or how little, of some events to include. The reception speeches, for example. It is best to record them in their entirety if possible and trim down later (if they prove boring or, dare we say it, inconsequential). You can guarantee that if you turn the camera off for a moment it will be the precise time that an absolute gem of a joke or quip is made – and those watching the video later will be waiting for that very moment.

posed shots don't always make for good movie footage but the process of
the photographer arranging bride and groom can be far more interesting!

Embellishment

The nature of digital video post-production is such that other
memorable elements can be included. There is often a wish,
both on the part of the families concerned and the video
producer, to include images from the still photographer's album,
either as a separate feature on the video or interspersed – at
appropriate points – with the live action. This can be
problematic, not from a technical point of view, but on account
of copyright. Though a wedding photographer is commissioned
(and paid) to take photographs of the event the copyright of
those photographs remains with the photographer (even though
ownership of the resultant prints and album is transferred to the
commissioner). Including photographs on the video will require
the copyright holder's permission.

Don't be surprised if, in giving permission, the photographer
applies a charge or conditions; his or her livelihood is based on
photographs of this and other events, and it is only natural that
he or she will want to gain maximum (but fair) benefit.

Cutaways and titles

You'll see from the list above that a number of cutaways are
suggested. These can be useful for truncating a service (when
hymns, for example, seem to go on forever, yet few guests seem
to be singing), while some, such as the wedding invitation,
provide the means of producing a title shot that is both easy to
arrange and includes an important element of the wedding. It's
useful to keep a pristine invitation just in case you need to shoot
some additional footage later, for example, as an accompaniment

to a special reading or prayer. If the sound is not sufficiently clear, a faded-in view of the text can help the audience of the video follow it more clearly.

an impromptu arrangement of props can make the ideal backdrop for a title shot

A child's birthday

Much of the mechanics of the wedding video can be translated to other social events such as children's parties. Such parties tend to follow a less rigorous order of events but nonetheless there are many scenes that characterize such events and will need to be recorded.

Where the party celebrates a child's birthday there's a tendency to concentrate only on the party itself – but some of the more magical scenes can be recorded throughout the day of the birthday. The child waking, opening presents and struggling to get to sleep at the end of a busy day all make for a memorable production. Follow the day through for an unforgettable recording. Party invitations or birthday cards can make excellent titles that are more appropriate (and easier) than adding titles during editing. Situations to consider for inclusions are:

- child waking (or waking parents or guardians)
- opening presents
- playing with presents
- party preparations
- guests arriving
- opening guests' presents
- games
- entertainer (if provided)

- singing and playing (to camera!)
- birthday lunch or tea
- bringing in the cake with lighted candles
- happy birthday chorus and blowing out candles (children will enjoy endless re-takes of this)
- guests leaving
- the final clear-up
- child off to bed.

If the party meal is likely to get messy as the children get increasingly covered in chocolate and jelly, remember to take plenty of cutaways to prevent absurd continuity errors.

party entertainers make great movie subjects
take some cutaways of the audience in case you need to shorten the performance

Celebration dinner

Whether for an older person's birthday, wedding anniversary or retirement, the train of events will be almost identical. In many ways a celebration dinner is similar to the wedding reception as we can see in the following scene suggestions:
- setting up the house or venue for the party
- location shots of the venue with cake and decorations
- guests arriving, with introductions if appropriate
- arrival of the guest of honour
- meal
- arrival of the cake
- blowing out candles/cutting the cake
- speeches
- partying.

Cutaways and titles

- the cake
- invitations
- place name cards.

Don't forget some exterior location shots of the venue – even if it is the guest of honour's home.

an after dinner singalong makes for great memories

a shot of the cake and a few balloons makes a perfect title that needs no words

The grand day out

The methodology of videoing the family day out is, by most criteria, quite unlike that of a wedding video. Though some scenes will be formulaic the majority will be impromptu. And, again, unlike the wedding video (where the video itself is almost obligatory), recording the day out should not impose too much on the event itself.

- packing the car
- checking the route on a map
- setting off
- the journey (can use 'stock' footage for this)
- arrival
- queuing to enter/go through ticket booth
- general views/establishing shots of location
- queuing for rides (at a theme park/fair ground)
- boarding ride
- on the ride
- establishing/location shots of the same ride to cut with the on-board footage
- audience and stage shots of entertainments

- departure
- journey home (with sleeping children).

a day at the beach can include events such as these windsurfers that are easily captured using the zoom lens (just watch out for the sand though!)

Cutaways and titles
- general views of park/theme park/venue
- entrance to park/theme park/venue
- people queuing for food and drinks
- family resting on benches.

getting there is part of the fun – so remember to capture it all on the video

18

Windows Movie Maker

In this chapter you will learn
- to navigate Windows Movie Maker
- how to create a movie with Movie Maker
- how to add sound and special effects.

Movie Maker, which is now an integral part of the Windows software portfolio, is a neat if basic movie manipulation application. Here's a brief guide to its operations and uses.

Interface

Windows Movie Maker has an interface that, after VideoWave and iMovie, should be somewhat familiar. Like these applications it is conveniently divided into working areas, in this case four.

- Toolbars: Like most Windows applications you can use the toolbars to perform commonly required tasks. Many of the buttons duplicate (and provide shortcuts to) menu items.
- Collections area: The organizational area for your video, audio and still images that have been recorded or imported.
- Monitor: The conventional monitor window previews the video, video clips or imported material. A scrubber bar (called seek bar here) can be used to move around the video, or you can use the conventional buttons below.
- Workspace: The workspace is where you can edit your movie. Like iMovie it features alternate storyboard or timeline views.

Movie Maker interface

Movie Maker filetypes

Movie Maker creates three principal file types from the media that you import and edit. These are:

- Project files: These contain all the information about the current editing project. The project will comprise video clips (or other media files) that you have added to the workspace. You do not have to complete the session in one go; you can save the project file and return later to perform some new, or different, edits. Project files are identified by the .mswmm extension.

- Movie files: The finished, saved movie becomes a movie file. Once created you can send it in an email, to a Web browser or write to a CD. Video only, or video and audio movie files, are saved as Windows Media files and given the .wmv file name extension. Those with audio only are given the alternate .wma extension.

- Collections file: The collections file is really a database file that stores databased information about your media collections. It contains information about the source files you import (though it does not contain the files themselves). It is important that this file is not deleted as to do so would render it impossible to track the component files pointed to by this file. You will recognize collections files by their .col file extensions.

Movie Maker, like contemporary products, enables movies to be produced in a few simple steps. In fact, four steps are all that is required:

1 adding content
2 editing a project
3 previewing the project
4 export the finished movie.

Adding content

Of course, before you can perform any edits you'll need to have some source material. In Movie Maker this involves importing material and converting it to Windows Media Format. Media files can be imported directly or by recording pre-recorded material sourced from a video camera, VCR or even television broadcasts. Source material can be digital, video or analogue. That material which you import will be displayed on the collections area. You can think of this as your store of raw footage from where you can start to organize that material. You can also record material from a digital (DV) camera or an analogue camera connected to an A to D converter in DV format. In this case the files are given an .avi file extension. You will need to connect in this case using a FireWire cable.

To configure your system for recording you'll need to specify the following:

- Source material type: you can choose to record video and audio together, audio only or video only.
- Capture device: If you have more than one capture device attached you'll need to select the required device. Note that if there is only one device attached that will be selected automatically.
- Quality: As ever you should aim to work at the highest quality possible, but do not exceed the quality of the capture devices (to do so would produce large file sizes without a commensurate increase in quality).
- Record time limit: The default maximum recording time is two hours but this may be reduced based on the hard disc space available for recording and the other settings you have made.
- Create clips: Select this to break your recording into separate video clips automatically. It functions in a similar way to the equivalent feature found in iMovie and VideoWave.

Recording from an analogue source

Here's how to import material from an analogue source such as an analogue VCR or camera.

1 Connect the source equipment and turn on. Start up Movie Maker.
2 Select File menu ➔ Record and select the source material type from the menu.
3 Check that the quality setting (in the Settings list) is set to the required setting and that the Record Time Limit is appropriate. Check that the Create Clips button is pressed (you'll probably want to leave it this way).
4 Start to play the source material and monitor playback in the monitor window of Movie Maker. Press the Record button at the start of the material you wish to record.
5 Click Stop when you reach the end of the recorded passage.
6 Save the recording with an appropriate filename.

Recording from a digital source

The process of recording from a digital source, such as a DV camera, is very similar.

1 Connect the camera using the FireWire connection and turn the camera to VCR (playback) mode.
2 Select File menu → Record. If your computer's processor speed is less than 600MHz it may not be fast enough to record in real time and a Warning dialogue box will appear. Click on Yes to proceed. You will have to evaluate, after recording, whether the process has been a success.
3 Use the Play and Record buttons in Movie Maker to review the tape in the camera and start the recording (you'll see the word 'Recording' blink while recording is in progress and the audio track, if there is one, will be supressed).
4 Click on Stop to finish recording.
5 Save the file as before.

Whether recording from a digital or analogue source you can create a movie file directly by selecting the Auto Generate File option. You will also find this option by selecting View → Options and then clicking on the Auto Generate File button.

You can also import files that are stored elsewhere on the computer. If they need to be converted you'll see a display such as that shown here illustrating the progress.

the progress of video conversion is shown by bar graphs. This may take some time, depending on the length of the video

Organizing imported material

Your imported material needs to be sorted and organized; you can do this using the Collections feature. Your clips will already be gathered together in the collections area. By default a thumbnail from each clip is displayed but you can choose to alternate displays such as a list view, which only displays a list of filenames. Remember that the corresponding collections file does not contain these media files and clips, it merely contains information about them and their whereabouts. Because of the importance of this file it makes good sense to back it up. Then, should it become corrupt, you have a working copy.

You can manipulate clips extensively. For example, you can move, rename, copy or delete them. You can add or modify properties such as the title, author, date, rating (an arbitrary rating system indicator) and description. You don't need to populate all these properties but it does help to organize them.

Editing

You have the same drag-and-drop functionality with Movie Maker that we've seen in iMovie and VideoWave. Pull them to the storyboard or timeline and you can assemble your movie on the desktop.

in storyboard view the clips are represented as thumbnails

a conventional timeline arrangement

You can trim a clip once it has been added to the timeline simply by dragging the trim handles to trim away the unwanted portions from the start or end of the clip. Note that the trimmed material is not shorn away; it remains in the source file so that it may be retrieved later if required. You can also split a clip either in the workspace window or while in the collections area.

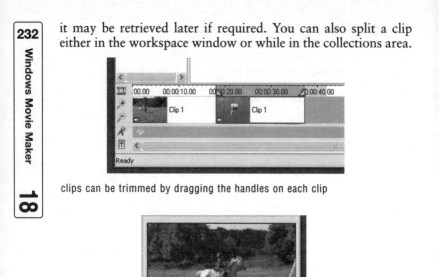

clips can be trimmed by dragging the handles on each clip

you can use the control button to split a clip at the appropriate point

Transitions are also added on the timeline. Click on the second of the clips that you want to place the transition between and drag it so that it overlaps the first. This overlap area, which is shown shaded, is the transition length.

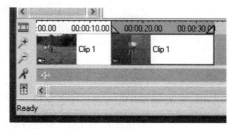

drag clips over each other to create transitions

Audio clips can be added and manipulated in the same way using the audio bar of the workspace. Again you need to be in timeline view to work. Audio transitions are slightly different in as much as overlapped audio tracks are each played at 50 per cent volume for the transitional period.

19

close: becoming a great movie director

In this chapter you will learn
- where to go for more information on software
- about websites offering help and information
- further sources of tutorial support.

It would be almost fatuous at this point to reiterate our earlier comments about how easy it is to edit digital video on the computer desktop. By now I hope you will have found out for yourself. But it is here that the adventure really begins. Now you'll need to develop your skills in the craft of movie making. Though we've given you a taster of what is possible nothing can beat the experience of discovering for yourself. Below, for added inspiration and advice, are some useful websites.

Software manufacturers' websites

You'll find more information about the software products, news on updates and useful support areas on the software manufacturers' websites. Some also include areas containing extra resources (such as sound effects, images or movie footage) or have useful links to companion sites.

VideoWave: www.roxio.com
iMovie: www.apple.com/imovie
VideoImpression: www.arcsoft.com
QuickTime: www.apple.com/quicktime
Premiere: www.adobe.com
Movie Maker: www.microsoft.com/windowsxp
Macromedia www.macromedia.com

Hardware manufacturers' websites

Many of the websites of hardware manufacturers feature important advice relating to their products, late breaking news and information with regard to getting the best out of them.

Canon: www.canon.co.uk
Casablanca (Hama): www.hama.co.uk
Formac: www.formac.com
Fujifilm: www.fujifilm.co.uk
Hauppage (USB A to D converters): www.hauppage.com
Iomega (storage): www.iomega.com
JVC: www.jvc.co.uk
Kodak: www.kodak.co.uk
Mitsubishi: www.meuk.mee.com
Panasonic: www.panasonic.co.uk
Sharp: www.sharp.co.uk
Sony: www.sony.co.uk (Sony Professional: sony-cp.com)
Toshiba: www.toshiba.com

Advice and tutorials

New websites relating to moviemaking, whatever your level of skill. Setting your favourite search engine to 'Movie Making' and 'Digital Video' will help locate a huge number of these. But here are a few of the better ones (please note, however, that Web addresses do change and that some can disappear altogether).

Techniques: www.simplydv.co.uk/techniques.html

Camcorder use: http://hometheater.about.com/cs/camcorders (there is also a large amount of general video and video editing advice on the About.com website).

Video camera use: www.videocamera.com.au

General tutorials: www.videouniversity.com

Short courses in digital video: www.shortcourse.com/video

General sites for digital video (including digital video editing) help and information

Here's a selection of general and specific sites relating to DV topics. They vary in scope from providing information to the beginner through to more specialized tips and help for the advanced digital worker.

www.dvcentral.com
www.dvhandbook.com
www.dvformat.com
www.dv.com
www.digitalproducer.com
www.webvideoguys.com

Further reading

Digital Video for Dummies, Martin Doucette, New York: IDG Books Worldwide, 2001

How to do Everything with Digital Video, Frederick H. Jones, Berkeley CA: McGraw Hill, 2002

The Complete Idiot's Guide to iMovie 2, Brad Miser, Que Books, 2001

Digital Video! I Didn't Know You Could Do That ..., Erica Sadun, Alameda CA: Sybex, 2001

The Little Digital Video Book, Michael Rubin, Berkeley CA: Peachpit Press, 2002

glossary

aliasing The production of *artefacts* when a signal is digitized, such as when a scene is recorded on digital video or an analogue signal converted. Most commonly seen as jagged 'stairstepping' on curved or diagonal lines.

analogue In video terms, any format or recording system that represents the intensity of a signal as a value that can be constantly varying. Compare with *digital* in which a discrete number represents all values composed of binary (0 and 1) code.

antialiasing Any process that reduces the effect of aliasing. Often involves averaging of brightness levels at sharp edges to achieve smoother (i.e. less jagged) transitions.

aperture The opening in a camera lens or lens assembly created by the iris diaphragm and adjustable (under automatic or manual control) to allow more or less light to reach the CCD sensor.

artefact Any image degradation brought about through the limitations of the video recording or reproduction process. Most commonly caused by data compression.

assemble edit Alternate name for linear editing wherein the original material is transferred from a camcorder (or video player) in the final sequence order to a video recorder. Also describes film (or, sometimes, videotape) editing where separate scenes are physically joined into the final sequence.

A to D conversion Analogue to digital conversion. The conversion of any analogue signal into a corresponding digital one. Used specifically to describe the conversion of analogue video to digital.

AVI Audio Video Interleave. Digital video format devised by Microsoft and used extensively in Windows and Windows applications. Microsoft, who now prefer to promote Windows Media/Direct Show technology, no longer support it.

batch capture The capture (to a video editing application, for example) of a batch of video clips. When a digital video is captured by an application the result is a batch capture as each scene is regarded a separate video clip.

batch digitizing The capture of analogue video clips in a sequence and conversion to a digital format. Usually uses the timecode recorded alongside the video signal to determine scene and recording breaks.

banding Video artefact that causes smooth gradients to be represented by stepped transitions and often caused as a result of compression.

Betacam SX Digital recording system (used by professional and semi-pro users) based on the tape used in the analogue Betacam SP format. Uses MPEG2 as the compression regime.

Blue screen Technique for combining a subject (usually studio based) with a background from a different source. The subject is first filmed in front of a plain coloured background (not necessarily blue). Later the colour is replaced with the background scene. Often called chroma keying.

broadcast quality An imprecisely defined term to describe any material (usually video programming) that has the picture quality and production quality to make it suitable for broadcast television. The term is also used to describe situations where only the picture quality matches that of broadcast video.

cache Memory in a computer reserved to speed certain components or actions, such as finding information on a hard disc.

capture The transfer of video footage to a computer hard drive. A conversion to digital form will be required as part of the process for a source that is analogue.

CCD Charge coupled device. In the context of video cameras, it is the light sensitized 'chip' that records the video signal. Both digital an analogue video camera (along with digital stills cameras) feature CCDs though in analogue cameras the output is converted to an analogue signal.

cDVD See *MiniDVD*.

Chromakey See *Blue screen*.

chrominance The colour component of a video signal. Contains information about the hue (colour) and saturation (amount of colour). Needs to be combined with a luminance (brightness) signal to produce a complete image.

clipping Distortion to an audio or video signal due to the volume or levels being too high for the processing equipment.

CMOS Acronym for Complementary Metal-oxide Semiconductor. A light sensor used in some digital cameras for recording image data. Compared with the alternate CCD sensors CMOS is more prone to electronic and optical noise and also to image errors. However, the lower price per unit makes them effective for lower priced cameras.

Codec Short for Compressor/Decompressor, a mathematical technique for rapidly compressing and decompressing sequences of images in a video. Popular codecs include MPEG1, MPEG2, MPEG4 and DV/.

colour saturation The amount of colour in a video signal.

component signal/video Video system in which the chrominance and luminance signals are handled separately to retain video quality. Used in digital and Hi-band analogue systems.

composite signal/video Video system in which *chrominance* and *luminance* signals are combined. Cheaper to implement but of lower quality than *component signal/video*.

compression The process of reducing the amount of data present in a data file. In digital video this means reducing the amount of data required to reproduce the video. Lossless compression achieves the reduction in file size without compromising image quality. Lossy compression results in some of the original data being lost; repeated opening and editing of a file under this regime can compound losses.

compression rate A measure of the degree of *compression* applied. Usually expressed as a compression ratio. Digital video (DV) formats reduce the file sizes by 80 per cent hence the compression ratio is 5:1.

compression ratio See *compression rate*.

Control-L An edit control system (used principally by Sony) to permit synchronized recording between a camera and video recorder. Tape movements can also be remotely controlled and synchronized. Control-L is a derivation of a system known as Lanc.

D-1 to D-9 Set of digital videotape standards for the recording of compressed and uncompressed, composite and component video. These do not correspond to consumer formats such as DV or MicroMV.

data rate The amount of data passed (through a broadcasting system, onto video tape or sent to/from a computer's hard disc) per second. As a general rule the higher the data rate the better the video quality.

Digital8 A consumer digital video format for recording digital video (DV) format video. Uses Hi-8 tape rather than a DV cassette but offers limited compatibility (i.e. playback) of Hi-8 and Video-8 tapes.

Digital Betacam Digital video format for professional use that uses mild 2:1 compression.

digital camera, digital stills camera Digital camera designed to take still pictures. Generally offer a resolution far superior to digital video cameras. Many models can record short movie clips using a much lower resolution than that normally used for photographs.

digitizer A board within a computer, or a peripheral device used to convert an analogue signal to a digital.

dissolve The process of dynamic mixing of one video source into another (giving the impression that the outgoing one is dissolving away).

driver Software application used to enable peripheral or installed devices (such as printers, soundcards and digitizers) work with the host computer.

DTV North American term for digital television, equivalent to *DVB* in the UK.

DV Digital Video. In capitalized form the specific format used in consumer digital video recording. Part of a family of similar formats that includes *DVCam* and *DVCPro*.

DVB Term used to describe digital television broadcasting (Digital Video Broadcasting) used mainly in the UK and Europe.

DVC Digital Video Cassette. Original name for the *DV* format.

DVCAM DV variant that uses (principally) a higher tape speed for improved quality recordings for the business market.

DVCPRO Panasonic's version of DV that runs tape 80 per cent faster for improved quality. Used extensively in the news gathering business.

DVCPRO50 Version of DVCPro that runs tape twice as fast and uses twice the data rate for high quality video.

DVD Digital Versatile Disc. A disc-based data storage medium that features a family of discs including DVD Video (video and movie material), DVD Audio (high quality audio), DVD-R (recordable DVD), DVD-ROM (data) and DVD-ROM (re-recordable). Note that not all DVD formats are equivalent or interchangeable.

DVE Acronym for digital video effects.

edit controller Hardware device (or computer software application) used to control the playback and recording of video (generally analogue) between two video decks.

Extra VideoCD, Extra VCD, XVCD An extension of the *VideoCD* format that stores video and audio using a non-standard bit rate. The result is higher picture quality but the format lacks the same degree of compatibility of VideoCD.

field One of two television images that are interlaced to produce a single 'frame'. In the *PAL* system, two fields of 312 lines, each displayed for 1/50 second produce the required 625-line/25 frames per second.

FireWire Name given by Apple for the IEEE1394 interface and communications protocol. Now used widely to describe the application of this in-digital video applications. It is widely used to download video from a camcorder to a computer and, being bi-directional, uploading edited video to the camera (acting as a recorder) or separate video deck.

FireWire card Card mounted inside a computer (or an appropriate peripheral) that supports the *FireWire* communication protocol.

generation loss The quality loss resulting from the copying of a video signal from one tape to another. Such a loss is described a single generation loss.

HDCAM High definition version of Digital Betacam. Used professionally, particularly for movie making.

HDTV High Definition Television. Strictly any television system offering resolution in excess of that offered by NTSC or *PAL*. Now usually applied to this when offered in widescreen (16:9) format.

Hi-8 Hi-band version of Video-8 used in camcorders from (principally) Sony and Canon.

Hi-band, High Band Analogue consumer video formats such as Hi8, SVHS and professional High Band Umatic in which the chrominance and luminance signals are processed separately to improve picture quality.

IEEE-1394 Systematic name for FireWire connections and systems.

i.Link Name used by Sony to describe its implementation of FireWire.

Interlace, Interlace Scanning The process in the creation of a conventional television or video picture of producing an image of 625 lines by first scanning the image with 312 lines for 1/50 second (the odd picture lines) followed by a similar number of even lines. The two add together to produce the full image frame. Each set of lines is known as a field. The alternative progressive scan builds the picture progressively.

interpolation The creation (in video production) of intermediate frames or components used to smooth signals or as part of the process of creating effects.

LANC See *Control-L*.

library Synonym for Shelf. An interface repository for video clips. Clips can be dragged from the library to the timeline to compile a movie.

linear editing Editing method where a new recording is compiled by copying original footage in the required sequence from video player.

lossless compression See *compression*.

lossy compression See *compression*.

luminance signal Component of a video signal that carries the brightness information (colour information is carried by the chrominance component).

Melzoic Type of television picture tube designed to operate at 100Hz but using advanced digital circuitry to prevent smearing artefacts sometimes visible on moving objects.

MicroMV Small digital video format devised by Sony that uses MPEG2 rather than DV as the recording format.

MiniDV Small video cassettes used in consumer DV camcorders. Distinguishes them from full sized DV cassettes used in professional decks.

MiniDVD A video recording format that uses MPEG2 data compression but records onto a standard DVD. Up to 20 minutes of DVD quality video can be stored on a CD though not all DVD players will replay MiniDVD discs.

M-JPEG   Acronym for Motion JPEG, Motion Joint Picture Experts Group. A specialized digital video compression process that delivers a data rate that varies with subject.

Mosquito Noise   Image artefact sometimes called feathering and represented by a 'buzzing' at transitional points in an image.

motion blocking   Artefact caused when the *data rate* used by a particular system is less than that required to reproduce a (usually fast-changing) scene. The image appears to break momentarily into small squares until the data rate can 'catch up'.

MOV   Video file format used in QuickTime.

MPEG   Acronym for Motion Picture Experts Group and the name of the compression standard they define. MPEG1 is used in VideoCD and offers quality similar to VHS on a standard CD. MPEG2 is used in the MicroMV format, DVB and DVD (although many variations exist). MPEG4 is a multimedia format. Further standards (such as MPEG7 and MPEG21 exist for specialized applications.

native editing   Editing that is conducted in the original format. Strictly applied, DV editing is not native (as it is decompressed for editing) but the term is often used for editing in a DV environment.

noise   Image (or audio) degrading signals that affect the original signal.

non-linear editing   Editing system in which a final sequenced video is compiled from individual video clips stored (usually) on a computer hard drive.

NTSC   Acronym for National Television Standards Committee. Also used to describe the analogue 525-line television system used in North America and Japan.

offline editing   Editing using copies of original footage (often made with cheaper media).

online editing   Editing using original, best quality media.

PAL   Acronym for Phase Alternation by Line. Television system used in the UK, most of Europe (except France and Russia) and many Commonwealth countries.

PALplus   Variant of *PAL* that can offer widescreen broadcasts and is compatible with conventional format televisions. Though broadcasts were funded by the EU for some time, it is essentially redundant in the face of *DVB*.

playhead   The point on a timebased representation of a video sequence indicating that part of the video currently being played.

playhead handles An alternate representation of the playhead comprising two triangular 'handles' that can be moved independently to define a section of a video clip for saving (cropping) or deleting (trimming).

Progressive scanning Video image scanning method where the image is built up in one continuous scan rather than the two interlaced scans of Interlace Scanning. Sharper individual images are possible but this can introduce some jerkiness to fast motion.

pixel Contraction of Picture Element, the smallest element of an imaging CCD and, by definition, the smallest element of the resulting image or video that can be recorded by the CCD.

QuickTime Apple's software application and system extensions for still and moving image and the automatic compression and decompression of the same. Included as part of the Macintosh operating system and available as a download for Windows. The Pro version (available at extra cost for both platforms) provides additional editing and transcoding features.

RAID Acronym for Redundant Array of Independent Discs. A specialized system of multiple 'managed' hard discs used to protect data against hardware failure.

resolution The amount of detail in a video image. The greater the resolution the greater the amount of detail that can be resolved. Video of lower resolution is generally smaller (in file size terms) than that of higher resolution.

rough cut A sequence of clips (or 'shots') assembled in approximate order to give a preview of a video based on trimmed clips.

saturation The amount of a particular colour in an image. The higher the saturation the brighter the colour; at zero saturation the image will be grey.

scrubber bar A timeline bar use in some image editing applications along which the playhead can be dragged to show the video image at that point. Trims and cuts can be made by dragging the playhead handles along this bar to define 'in' and 'out' points.

SECAM Acronym for Sequential Couleur Avec Memoire. Television standard used in France, Russia and former territories of each. Uses the same 625-line/25 frames per second as *PAL*.

sequence A collection of video clips assembled in approximate order to enable an assessment of the order and further editing requirements to be made.

Shelf   The area in the iMovie interface (and some other applications) used to store video clips (or, rather, thumbnail representations). Clips can be dragged from the shelf to the timeline and dragged back again.

standards conversion   The conversion of a TV signal between different broadcast standards, such as between the UK *PAL* standard and the North American *NTSC*.

storyboard   A layout used when devising a filming sequence. Uses rough pictorials (along with descriptive captions) of scenes to give an impression of the shots needed to tell a story or illustrate a subject. Also a term used to describe a very basic timeline where video clips are represented by thumbnails. Rather than showing the duration of each clip this merely illustrates the sequencing.

streaming video   Very highly compressed video that is transmitted over the Internet and replayed in real time or near real time as the download continues (rather than being downloaded in its entirety prior to replay).

subpixel   An image element smaller than a pixel. When detailed special effects are required they need to be applied (or rendered) at the subpixel level to ensure that the quality of the effects are reduced by working at pixel level.

Super Video CD, Super VCD, SVCD   Extension of the *VideoCD* format that offers up to 30 minutes of moderate (better than VHS) quality video on a standard CD.

S video   The connection provided on Super VHS and Hi-8 VCRs, camcorders and peripherals that carries the brightness (luminance) and colour (chrominance) signals separately, delivering higher quality, cleaner video.

timecode   Coded information added to videotape to define a frame precisely in terms of time and frame numbering. Timecode information can be added to analogue video using appropriate cameras or editing equipment. All digital formats include timecode information as part of the respective format specification.

timeline   Interface feature of video editing software used to represent the structure of a movie. Video clips are displayed as horizontal bars with lengths corresponding to their duration. Additional video and audio tracks can also be displayed. In some video editing applications a simpler *storyboard* representation is used.

Video-8 Consumer video format devised by Sony using small cassettes (around the size of an audio cassette) containing 8-mm-wide tape. Also used advanced (for its time) pulse code modulation sound recording for improved audio quality.

VideoCD, Video Compact Disc Video recording format used initially with CD-I (CD Interactive) systems to compress around one hour's video (at VHS quality) on to a conventional CD. Little used commercially except in the Far East. Using the *MPEG1* format, VideoCDs can be produced by many video-editing applications and played on most DVD players.

video editing application Software designed for *non-linear editing* of video material.

white balance Camera setting that adjusts the colour balance so that white and neutral objects are correctly rendered under different lighting sources. Most cameras now feature automatic white balance controls that alter the balance according to the ambient conditions but these – and others – also have manual controls that can be preset for daylight, tungsten light, fluorescent light, overcast skies and more.

windows media file Any file containing audio, video, or script data that is stored in Windows Media Format. File extensions including: .asf, .asx, .wax, .wm, .wma, .wms, .wmv, .wmx, or .wvx are used depending on the content or purpose of the files.

XVCD See *Extra VCD*.

index